D0945403

Lean Manufacturing in

BUILD TO ORDER

*Complex and Variable
Environments*

Lean Manufacturing in

BUILD TO ORDER

*Complex and Variable
Environments*

by

*Jorge L. Larco
Elena Bortolan
Michael H. Studley*

THE OAKLEA PRESS

RICHMOND, VIRGINIA

ISBN 10: 1-892538-41-5
ISBN 13: 978-1-892538-41-3

If your bookseller does not have this book in stock,
it can be ordered directly from the publisher.
Contact us for information about discounts
on quantity purchases.

The Oaklea Press
6912 Three Chopt Road, Suite B
Richmond, Virginia 23226

Voice: 1-800-295-4066
Facsimile: 1-804-281-5686
Email: Info@OakleaPress.com

This book can be purchased online at

http://www.LeanTransformation.com

CONTENTS

Acknowledgments

Work on this book began at a retreat in Sioux City, Iowa, at a hotel overlooking the wide Missouri in January 2006, where we spent the weekend with our editor and publisher discussing and outlining its scope and content. Since then many long hours have been spent and e-mails have darted back and forth around the globe, supplemented by transatlantic and intercontinental phone calls, as the manuscript grew in size and passed through a lengthy series of drafts.

We are indebted to those who reviewed the drafts and offered expert input, advice and ideas, including our friend Lucio Colussi, Vice President and Category Leader, Acrylic & Wellness Ideal Standard, and Kurt Kefgen a senior and knowledgeable member of our team who contributed in the writing of the metrics chapter. We are also indebted to our co-author of *Lean Transformation* and *A Workbook for Assessing your Lean Transformation,* Bruce Henderson, former CEO of Imation Corporation, who always provides us with enthusiastic, profound and challenging ideas to pursue. Of course, the book would not have become a reality without the help, encouragement and strong support of our editor and publisher, Stephen Hawley Martin.

Our thanks also go to many of our clients, who contributed with their encouragement, commitment and trust to enable us to help them transform their highly variable, complex Build-to-Order businesses into Lean Enterprises.

We offer our thanks to each and all of them.

Foreword

by

Bruce A. Henderson
Former Chairman & CEO,
Imation Corporation

Hats off to Jorge Larco, Elena Bortolan, and Mike Studley for charting new territory in the global movement to adopt Lean manufacturing. Before publication of the book you now hold, most people involved in high-variability manufacturing were able only to dream of reaping the full benefits of Lean production. That now has changed.

Many experts thought what the authors set out to accomplish was impossible. After all, Toyota and its disciples preach level scheduling and standard processes, simple enough to adhere to in many industries, but not so in those where volatile demand, constantly changing volumes and widely varying processing times are the norm. Many a manufacturer facing such challenges has given Lean a try and come to the conclusion, "It just doesn't work in my business."

Rather than throw in the towel, however, Larco and his team have embraced the need for variable product processes and assembly paths and overcome the obstacles, providing a methodology for reassigning material, people and machinery daily, or even hourly when necessary. The result is a brand new playing field.

To meet the constantly changing demands of customers in a dynamic marketplace, the authors have combined the principles of Lean with computerized algorithms in a way not done before, creating a new Lean paradigm for businesses operating in highly variable, complex manufacturing environments. As Larco and his associates have demonstrated, the impact on companies in such environments is huge. One can expect a reshuffling of competitive standings to occur and winners and losers to emerge not imagined or anticipated today.

The winners will be companies with leaders who recognize that Lean is not just operational, it is strategic, and employ the techniques described in this book to their fullest potential. It is no accident, for example, that Toyota has surpassed all others to become the largest auto producer in the world.

Nowadays, a business that can deliver a high-quality, customized product at a low price — and do so when the customer wants — stands a good chance not only of staying in business, but of being a leader of its category. In the past, this was possible only in certain industries where repetition was the norm. Now, thanks to Larco, Bortolan, and Studley, it is possible in highly variable, complex manufacturing environments as well.

Introduction

When the book *Lean Transformation* was published in 1999, our primary goal was to create a tool that would explain in simple, everyday language the basic concepts and practices of Lean Production. We wanted to show practical examples of Lean Enterprises in action. At that point in time, what constituted a Lean Enterprise was just beginning to be known by managers of businesses around the world. Many companies located in the United States were already starting to implement Lean concepts, and a few companies in Europe were beginning to experiment with them.

Today, most leaders of businesses of average size or larger have at least some experience with Lean. Based on what we know and have seen, we can say with confidence that leaders in more than 50% of the companies around the developed world have read about, discussed and implemented at least a few Lean concepts.

Initially, the driving factors were the needs to reduce costs, to be more efficient, and to offer higher levels of service than competitors in an effort to gain market share and to grow a business. For these reasons, most of the Lean transformations we were undertaking at that time, were related to production.

Today's market challenges

From the turn of the century to the present day, the world has evolved rapidly, and the customers have become ever more demanding. Whatever your business, it seems as though everyone wants something a little different. Customers in today's competitive, global marketplace want their goods and services to be of the highest quality, the lowest cost, customized to their specific needs, and they also have specific delivery requirements. This has led companies across the globe to adopt the Toyota Production System, also known as Lean Manufacturing, because it allows them to turn out the highest quality products at the lowest possible costs, and to deliver them quickly using pull-scheduling — meaning products are not produced until an order for them is received.

But what if the products your company makes are complex and are offered to your customers in many different variations? Most people think that implementing continuous flow, JIT (Just-In-Time) manufacturing isn't all that difficult for companies stamping out identical widgets, but they believe that using this strategy in a complex manufacturing environment may be virtually impossible. After all, complex products present a host of challenges and offering them in different variations seems to make Lean processes impractical. However, this is not the case, which is why we have written this book. We want to show you examples and offer you a number of practical approaches to implementing

Lean in highly variable, engineered-to-order environments.

In such environments, establishing and maintaining flow is an important goal in the Lean journey, and it's true that the scheduling of complex and variable products through the assembly process can be an extremely challenging task. But we have found that it can almost always be accomplished using the right production approaches coupled with assistance from evolved scheduling tools and software. This will be dealt with in detail in a chapter dedicated to this subject.

Nowadays, a company that can deliver a high quality customized product at a low price — and do so when the customer wants it — stands a good chance of becoming a leader in their industry because such an offer is hard to beat.

When you think about it, most successful companies got that way because they presented potential customers with an irresistible offer. Take Federal Express, a $27 billion company so essential nowadays that corporate America might grind to a halt if FedEx and its competitors who followed in that company's footsteps ceased operations. It all began with an idea laid out in a Yale undergraduate term paper authored by founder Fred Smith, which according to popular lore received a C from his skeptical professor. The company filled a huge need at the time because the monopolistic United States Postal Service provided unacceptable results to a lot of really important people on Wall Street, Madison Avenue and in business centers across America. FedEx became essential by making an offer businesses in a hurry couldn't refuse — guaranteed overnight delivery.

"When it absolutely, positively has to be there overnight" was the advertising slogan. About the only thing this doesn't communicate is price. If the price hadn't been right, FedEx would not have blasted off. But in the early days, price wasn't the first question a businessman or woman asked if it really, absolutely, positively had to be there the next morning.

What about you? Suppose you could deliver just the right goods faster than any of your competitors? Nowadays, people want what they want when they want it, so it makes sense to offer speed and customization.

But there's another factor in today's marketplace that must be considered: the ongoing pressure to reduce prices. This is especially true when a company has been supplying another business with certain parts or components for some time. After a while, the company that's being supplied expects the price of an item to go down. This has frequently led to "de-localization" because one way to lower prices has been to move production to a different country where the cost of labor is lower. But calculating the savings based on lower labor costs alone can be misleading. Moving production offshore to a low-cost-labor country may not provide the competitive advantage hoped for when every angle is considered.

Many Times It Is Better to Go Lean Than to Go Abroad

An option that may need to be considered is whether it may be more convenient to transform into a Lean Enterprise and in this way optimize the company's resources in an existing location. This may be particularly wise if a company is looking at relatively low volumes coupled with the need to offer product customization and rapid delivery. It may be possible to fulfill these requirements at a distance, but shipping times, shipping costs, the issues associated with engineering a particular customer need, as well as potential quality issues ought to be carefully considered. A case in point is presented by a company we worked for that has a plant in Romania. Before this country joined the European Union, it took two weeks for the product made there to be shipped to Hungary, even though Hungary is only four hours away from Romania by car. Why? Customs and other complicated legal issues made it time consuming to deliver products between the two countries.

Our experience has been that in most cases a significant competitive advantage can be realized if a plant can deliver customized products in close proximity to its customers. De-localization may make sense if the company plans to serve the new local market as well as the old, but de-localization simply to take advantage of lower labor costs may only make sense in certain cases. Consider the examples of Toyota and Dell, two highly-successful Lean producers. Dell has three manufacturing facilities in the United States, as well as plants in China, Brazil, Malaysia, and Ireland. Toyota has more than 50 manufacturing operations located in more than two dozen countries, including the United States. These companies are able to make products efficiently and remain highly competitive with manufacturing plants across the globe serving the markets in proximity to them.

The Future is Lean

High customization, low cost, quick turnaround, and ever diminishing volumes is the future. But how does a company accomplish this and still be Lean?

Perhaps you build something really complicated such as trucks, houses, trailers, airplanes, machinery, automobiles, commercial heating and air conditioning equipment, or any of hundreds or maybe even thousands of products that have practically an infinite number of ways they can be configured. And perhaps some configurations call for features or subassemblies that can add many hours to a build, thus hopelessly throwing off the cadence of an assembly line. How can highly variable, complex products such as these be manufactured in a Lean environment?

The products mentioned can and already are being built to order in Lean environments. For manufacturers to adapt means the layout of lines and processes must take into account the many variations of a product that customers may require. Additionally, since volumes often are small — the minimum quantity may be as little as one — it is usually not possible to have a dedicated line for a particular product. More and more often companies need a universe of machines that can be employed in many different combinations to produce a large variety of highly customized products.

In the past, specialized products generally cost considerably more than standard models off the shelf, but this is not always true today. To be profitable and competitive, a company must find efficient ways to build products to order. As you read ahead, strategies and tactics will be offered that will help you take advantage of the trend toward customization and heightened customer expectations. Whatever your industry, whether it's apparel, electronics, consumer products, white goods, industrial products, or anything and everything in between, the issues are similar, and the solutions are the same — at least conceptually.

Every company has its own needs and particularities, of course, so the implementation of the concepts presented in this book should be tailored to the specific situation. For example, we have helped sister companies producing the same kinds of product, but located in different countries, go Lean. Based on cultural considerations and design differences in the products made, slightly different models worked best in each.

Chapter One: Lean Manufacturing in a Highly Variable Environment

First, let's paint a picture of a Lean Enterprise in a build-to-order, complex assembly environment. As mentioned, it's one characterized by the production of short lots — orders may be as small as one item — of diverse products that may be manufactured once in a while, once a year, or just once and never again. In this environment, some of the basic rules of Lean must be viewed in a different light. Standardized work is a requirement. However, with high variations, it may be tricky to determine what to standardize and how to layout the lines to ensure that flow of value-added activities is continuous. Balancing may not always be possible, or even practical. If products are made only once and never again, the cost of balancing may be prohibitive. And flowing may have to be carefully scheduled, sometimes with the use of a software-supported scheduling process. As will be discussed in detail, daily scheduling is an important element in the application of Lean manufacturing to complex and variable, build-to-order environments and many times it will need the help of dedicated software. Nevertheless, all the basic Lean concepts can be applied. Their applications may be slightly different, however, than would be the case in a traditional environment.

This book will walk you through the various challenges faced by companies that have the characteristics indicated above, and it will assist you in choosing the strategies and tactical options that enable a company like yours to apply Lean principles and compete effectively. To begin, we would like to summarize the basic elements of a Lean Enterprise so that we can use them in our journey to implement Lean Manufacturing in highly variable, build-to-order environments.

Lean Principles

Lean principles and practices need to be followed and applied in order to affect a Lean transformation. The six principles of the complete Lean program can be viewed as tools or pillars that support and work together to create a Lean operation. They need to be applied systematically to manufacturing as well as to other parts of the organization. We've found that leaders often make the mistake of implementing only one or two, but all are required to fully transform a traditional business into a Lean Enterprise.

In the book *Lean Transformation* we thoroughly described the six basic principles of Lean Production, referring to their application primarily in a repetitive environment. Here we would like to revisit them briefly and to highlight the main differences in the application of each in a highly variable environment. (Also, see Figure 1, page 20.)

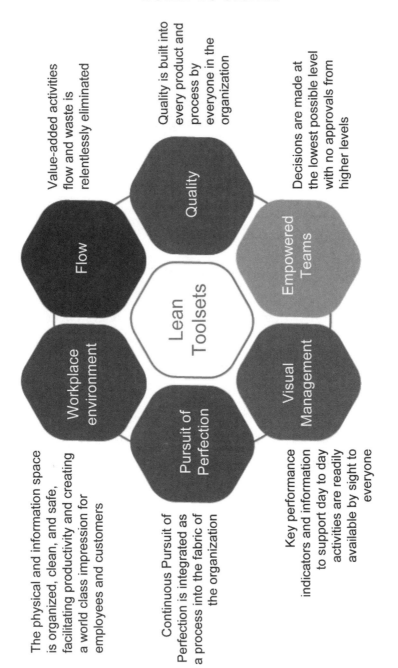

Value-added activities flow and waste is relentlessly eliminated

Quality is built into every product and process by everyone in the organization

Decisions are made at the lowest possible level with no approvals from higher levels

The physical and information space is organized, clean, and safe, facilitating productivity and creating a world class impression for employees and customers

Continuous Pursuit of Perfection is integrated as a process into the fabric of the organization

Key performance indicators and information to support day to day activities are readily available by sight to everyone

Flow

Quality

Empowered Teams

Lean Toolsets

Workplace environment

Pursuit of Perfection

Visual Management

Fig. 1 — The six priniciples of a Lean operation

Workplace Safety, Order, and Cleanliness

Studies show that the quality of a workplace directly correlates with the quality of the products being produced. This is not a coincidence. A sloppy environment subliminally communicates to those who work in it that is all right to be sloppy. It is why, above all, a Lean workplace must be safe, orderly, and immaculately clean. Picture a hospital operating room. This is what it should be like. The factory area should be brilliantly lit — as bright as daylight. All surfaces will have a fresh coat of paint, including walls, floors, machines and counter tops. Every piece of equipment, every tool, every storage bin or cart in an area should have its own special place and this place should be indicated by a painted or taped outline of the object. When not in the hands of a worker, these objects will be safely stowed. All potential safety hazards will have been eliminated, including wires and

Fig. 2 — Workplace safety, order and cleanliness, an example

extension cords. Everything will meet or exceed government safety standards.

Just-In-Time (JIT) Production

A Lean producer normally manufactures its products only to customer demand, not to forecasts or "to stock." In highly variable environments, however, particularly those with a good deal of seasonality, a need may exist to produce up to a predetermined point and store this for use later on. For products that are customized according to customer preferences, for example, production to stock will often be completed up to the stage just before customization normally would begin. Alternatively, subassemblies and other materials or components may be built and stored. This issue will be discussed at greater length in the upcoming chapter.

When a customer order is received, engineering may be required as well as a determination of any special parts that might be needed. Once this is done, certain steps will be followed to assure on-time delivery. The order will come under the direction of the daily scheduler and await its turn in a queue before entering final assembly.

This is slightly different than a typical line-produced product. Usually, an order for such a product can be sent directly to the final assembly line to await its turn. But in a highly variable environment in which products must navigate a universe of machines, the scheduling of the product through the various phases is critical. For example, subassemblies need to be scheduled in advance in order to arrive in a timely manner at the place they will be needed.

The sequence of items to be produced will be according to an established priority, which usually is determined by the date a customer has requested delivery. If necessary, the assembly line will be changed over in seconds or minutes to meet the requirements of a new order, and production will be completed according to the established takt time for the particular product and line configuration.

A key objective of a JIT producer is to manufacture its products in a continuous flow process, ideally without any breaks or interruptions in the flow. It is important to understand, however, that in highly variable environments this may not always be possible. Even though flow remains a basic and fundamental goal, such a producer may not have enough machines of a certain type or may have insufficient machine capacity to be compatible with true flow. Therefore, buffers, that expand and contract like accordions, may be set up in front of particular processes. During the early part of a shift, the buffer may be full. As the day progresses, the buffer will become depleted, only to be filled again for the next process cycle — most likely with a different type of subassembly.

It is important to properly balance lines so that every activity in the process flows at the same rate. If process A takes two minutes, process B should take two minutes, and so forth. Some processes, however, must be uncoupled from the production line, especially in situations where high capacity (fast) equipment is already in existence at a facility and must be used. Uncoupling may also be necessary in order to link in operations that are inherently batch processes such as injection molding, stamping or plating.

As previously noted, in some highly variable, non repetitive environments, balancing may not be practical. If a product is going to be made only once, for example, balancing may not be practical. The effort might simply be too costly to justify.

Another important aspect is Standardize Work. However, there is a need to determine a specific application of standardized work to this type of highly variable, build to order environment. We discuss this important issue further along in this book.

All of these issues do not mean that Lean principles cannot be employed or that flow cannot be applied. It means that Lean methods that are normally part of a systematic production process may not work and that other Lean methods must be used. These issues will be specifically addressed.

Kanban

JIT production employs Kanban, a production control system that enables Lean companies to better manage the manufacturing of products. Kanban is specifically designed for a "pull" as contrasted to the traditional "push" scheduling approach. There are three fundamental components, (1) an "indicator" that shows what part, component or subassembly is required, in what quantities, who will use it, and where it is stored; (2) a "signal" that indicates when an action is required, which in turn enables the fulfillment process to be prioritized; and (3) a clearly defined and systematic process assuring fulfillment in accordance with the indicator and signal.

Kanbans are used to "pull" components and materials into final assembly operations on replenishment, or on a one-time basis. When a replenishment Kanban is in place, a signal is sent to the upstream operation — or to an outside supplier — to produce and send the exact quantity of components or materials called for by the Kanban. Such a Kanban is sent each time the quantity called for has been consumed. In this way only the amount actually needed is produced.

A one-time Kanban is typically used in case of non-repetitive production. For example, a one-time Kanban might be a signal calling for the production of parts for a one-time, non-repeating order. When production of the parts has been completed and they have been delivered as called for, the Kanban has served its purpose and is eliminated.

In a Lean Enterprise, inventory is viewed as an "evil" that hides problems. So, a key objective of a JIT operation is to run with as little inventory as possible, while still being able to maintain the level of service goal a company has set in order to meet customers' needs. Using Kanbans helps to reduce inventory and to keep the level under control.

In highly variable environments, a semi-repetitive part or component may sometimes suddenly experience a spike in demand. If the spike is bigger than the Kanban, or if it uses all the Kanban at one time, a stock outage may result. When this happens, a supplier may be asked to replenish the Kanban in a time shorter than has been agreed upon. To prevent this, the scheduler, using specific software tools, should be able to predict this event and release a one time Kanban for the quantity needed to cover the spike. This ought to be scheduled like a normal work order because material and capacity availability need to be carefully evaluated before an order confirmation is sent to the customer. Of course, a longer lead time than normal may be required. If the customer cannot accept this delay, the existing Kanban can still be used. In addition, if we know spikes will occur during the year, a safety stock can be added into the calculation of the total Kanban quantity to cover for these.

As we often say, Kanban calculation and the implementation of a Kanban system seem easy but they require a good deal of knowledge and experience because of the many and variable factors that need to be considered and the rules that need to be established. These may include how to set up replenishment rules, the periodical maintenance of Kanban levels, space available in the shop floor, number of different lines using the same component/part at the same time, and so forth.

Additional factors and techniques normally associated with JIT production need to be taken into consideration as well. In particular, rapid changeovers are critical to avoid the need for excessive inventory between operations and to reduce lot sizes. These changeovers are often referred to as Single Minute Exchange of Die, or SMED. When thinking of setups, it's interesting to consider the impact they can have in areas beyond the factory floor. Imagine the negative impact changeovers can have on the productivity of an office. Each time a phone rings, the person receiving the call must interrupt an activity. The call requires attention, and a process needs to be set up in order to give an answer. Sometimes a call may have nothing to do with what a person is working on that day. This means a new setup is required on the new subject, and later, another setup on the activity that was interrupted at the time of the call. If production areas worked like offices, the concept of flow would be out the window. There are many solutions to this issue such as the recorded menu greeting that funnels callers into categories that can be quickly handled by workers already set up and prepared to take calls on specific topics.

Total Productive Maintenance Saves Time and Money

Total Productive Maintenance (TPM) plays a critical role since unexpected breakdowns of machines can cripple or stop the flow of an assembly line. An important objective is for machines and fixtures to work well when needed so that potential stoppages do not interrupt the production process.

Rather, a maintenance schedule should be part of the factory routine so that preventive maintenance takes place at times that will not disrupt the production process and machines work as they should, when they should.

Six Sigma Quality

Six Sigma is a phrase coined by Motorola to represent its drive for a very low failed parts per million rate. Six Sigma represents a mathematical calculation, 99.9996% perfection. This figure equates to 3.4 ppm (failed parts per million), or very close to zero defects. A Lean producer designs and builds Six Sigma quality into its products and processes, rather than merely "inspecting" for quality. Lean producers have superb root-cause problem solving skills and relentlessly pursue quality problems until they cannot occur again — often using mistake-proofing techniques (referred to as "Poka Yoke" in Japanese). Quality departments focus on quality "assurance," defect prevention and defining and promoting the company's quality culture, not on inspection. In fact, most Lean producers have eliminated quality inspectors. Instead, the factory floor operators are fully responsible for the quality of the products they make.

Workforce Empowerment

A Lean organization is much less hierarchical than a traditional company. In other words, it will be flatter, having fewer layers of management. Lean producers strive for an empowered workforce, organized into teams that are authorized to make decisions in a team's work area of responsibility.

Individual team members and their associates are empowered to make critical, on-the-spot decisions. A question might be raised, for example, does product quality meet the customer's standards? If it does not, production will be stopped until the situation can be corrected.

A culture of accountability and empowerment is even more important in highly variable environments than in those that are repetitive in nature. In many cases, for example, it may not be possible for Engineering to have detailed all aspects of a design. As a result, some aspects of an assembly may be left to the discretion of workers. Having said this, we are not suggesting that incomplete drawings or those with critical quotes missing are acceptable. Whatever is needed to assure the quality of the product should be included in its design. Nevertheless, if an empowered-team environment does not exist, problems that arise on a daily basis will not be resolved on the spot as they otherwise would be. We all know the boss cannot be everywhere at once, but nonetheless, the company will come to a standstill until he/she gets there, and valuable time and money will be lost.

Visual Management

A Lean factory is a visual factory. Management is by sight, not by computer listings. The objective is to have

BUILD TO ORDER

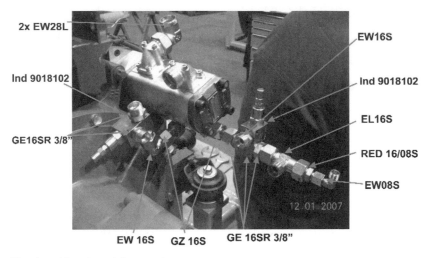

Fig. 3 — Visual work instructions

timely, complete and accurate information available for those who need it when they need it. This means putting real-time information in the hands of the entire workforce at all times, including information about orders, production schedules and progresses, quality, delivery performance versus customer want dates, and the financial health of the business. This information is collected and displayed on workcell bulletin boards, kiosks, and other easily-seen media.

In many companies, inventory information is hidden away and available only to those who can access a computer screen and have proper authority. In the Lean factory, inventory is organized so that it can be seen visually.

Andon lights and display boards are used to signal machine breakdowns, material shortages, and other production problems.

Visual instructions should also be used to show operators how to assemble a product or its subassemblies (see fig. 3).

Visual instructions are easier to understand than written instructions and take less time.

In general, someone walking onto a Lean shop floor should be able to tell the status of operations within a few minutes, just by looking around.

A key fundamental in building houses, large stationary equipment or other complex assemblies is to create a sense of flow, visually. In the case of a complicated piece of machinery, for example, the stage of construction that's been reached may be difficult to determine simply by looking. Yet cell leaders and workers as well as scheduling and materials management may need to know. They shouldn't put up the wallboard, for example, until the house has been wired. But just as everyone in a small town instantly knows how close the United Way goal is to being reached the moment they pass the colored-in thermometer erected in town square, construction progress can be communicated instantly by coloring in a Gantt chart of construction activities laid out in the proper sequence.

Continuous Pursuit of Perfection

Lean producers never give up trying to achieve perfection, such as zero defects, 100% on time delivery, minimum to zero inventory, absolute lowest cost, and the most innovative designs. A constant and widespread focus exists on eliminating "muda" in all forms, muda being the Japanese word for waste.

BUILD TO ORDER

In a highly variable environment, one where repetitive building of products is limited, it's frequently necessary for operators to have to determine the most effective and efficient way to organize their work. The goal is to achieve flow and thus increase efficiency while meeting customer delivery dates. Trial and error, practice and involvement are required for this to take place. As such, the continuous improvement process needs to be a way of life. It should be felt, enjoyed and fostered by everyone involved.

Beyond the Lean Producer: The Lean Enterprise

The six toolsets, when applied consistently, will result in a Lean producer. To be a Lean Enterprise, however, it is necessary to go beyond the production floor in order to implement the six toolsets throughout the organization. Management needs to review the company's structure, culture and management style, and to take the steps necessary to empower the company's support functions to change.

What are the characteristics of a Lean Enterprise?

The entire organization functions as a team. No physical or metaphorical walls should exist between departments. Waste has been banished not only on the shop floor but also in the offices so that information now flows freely between departments and individuals. Value-added activities flow without interruption. Areas of the business such as sales, human resources, product engineering, and process engineering work in concert to create value for customers.

Fig. 4 — *Lean Enterprise:* a company where Lean Production principles have been applied to the entire organization and to the external value chain.

Relationships are built with suppliers with these same goals in mind. Supplier support and proximity have, for example, been important factors in Dell Computer's success. Even accounting will have to adapt by developing a system to measure the financial results and benefits of the changes brought about by the company's Lean transformation.

Recap

Just-in-time production to customer pull is a key aspect of a Lean producer. Continuous flow is an important aspect of this in both a repetitive environment as well as one that is build-to-order. In the latter, this is accomplished by determining the bottlenecks that will be created by the mix of products to be produced in a given period of time and scheduling the production sequence in a way that will minimize these bottlenecks. Often, anticipated bottlenecks can be scheduled to offset one another. Also, alternate routing through the various workstations can be mapped out so that products continue flowing. Often a product will pass by others requiring more steps.

Daily scheduling is an important facet of Lean manufacturing in a complex and variable, build-to-order environment. In addition to just-in-time production and flow, the other tools of Lean production ought to be put to work. These include workplace safety, order and cleanliness because shoddy environments can be expected to turn out shoddy products, and a high-quality environment can be expected to result in high-quality products.

Other tools include Kanban, which is a production control system that results in parts, components and materials being available where they are needed, when they are needed, in the quantity they are needed. Six Sigma quality is built into the Lean producers' products by using mistake proofing techniques. Quality inspectors are not necessary because everyone is responsible for the quality of his or her own work. Moreover, the Lean workforce is empowered to make decisions. Teams can decide what needs to be done in their respective areas. In addition, information is readily available and widely shared. A Lean factory is a visual factory. Signs and charts show hourly progress. The attitude that permeates the Lean producer is one of constant striving for improvement and perfection.

Chapter Two: Layout and Factory Design

It's essential when designing a Lean manufacturing facility to fully understand what the facility will need to accomplish. This requires a solid projection of the products and quantities the market will require the facility to build. The goal is to match market and production takt time, i.e., the pace of consumption of the products in the marketplace as well as the actual production pace required to meet this demand.

Designing an operation that always works the same way day in and day out is not as tricky as designing a build-to-order facility for complex and variable products. In such a plant, not all products are likely to be routed through every machine. Typically, a configuration is worked out that allows products to take alternate routes, some passing through one machine, some through another, and perhaps all products through a third or a fourth machine based on customization needs. The sequence of products to be assembled and their routing schedule on a given day will depend on the mix of products to be made that day. Scheduling and balancing become critical issues in such a setup. Operators often must move from one station to another and be multi-skilled. They have to have sufficient knowledge to balance their work and maintain flow.

As has been discussed, the marketplace we find ourselves in today requires more and more customization of products.

This trend has led to smaller lot sizes and shorter runs. Not long ago the trend was toward automation. A goal was to cut labor costs. Costs were transferred from variable to fixed, in other words, from people to highly automated machines. This may have seemed wise at the time. But now some executives regret having made that move because the more automated a plant's machines are, the more difficult it usually is to adapt the operation to small lots and product customization, as well as to the constant and increased need for maintenance. In a variable market, smaller equipment that can be moved easily and is designed for flow is almost always preferable. For one thing, it is easier to adapt to new situations. Also, with smaller and lower cost equipment, it may make sense to purchase additional machines so that parallel lines, or alternate routings, can be set up to run more than one product at a time.

Designing the Factory Layout

Before the design process can begin, a need exists to determine what the facility will be required to produce. Three factors should be considered: the first is where the market has been — the historical record of what has been produced; second is where the market is headed, or what trends suggest the number and mix of various products will be in the future; and third, what the strategic objectives are of the company.

We usually begin by analyzing marketplace needs for the

various products and configurations customers may require. We look at which products have been produced in the past and in what quantities, and we attempt to determine where the market is headed in order to gauge the future demand for each. This appears to be simple and easy enough, and certainly sales and marketing should have a good feel for where things are headed. We have found in many cases, however, that feelings and reality don't turn out to be in sync. It is best to focus on a clear picture of what has really happened during the past few years, and in a focused way, challenge those closest to customers to consider fully how the market and competition will react to the availability of products based on a different service level — one with shorter lead times and more flexibility in terms of what is being offered, especially in the area of customization.

Invariably, we will conclude that some products will be produced frequently, and others only occasionally. In some environments a line of products may have certain variations, or be made available with different options, and the approximate cycle times are similar. In the same company, other products may provide similar functionality but have important design differences and different cycle times, making them substantially different in terms of manufacturing complexity. These products may be manufactured once in a while, once and never again or, in certain cases, they may be manufactured periodically. In some of theses cases, we may be able to design one line that handles all products as well as

The steps in a highly variable environment

1. Fully understand what the facility will need to accomplish:
   a. Where the market has been
   b. Where the market is headed
   c. The strategic objectives of the company

2. Determine volumes by product or family of products

3. Determine the various takt times

4. Define: # of stations required, labor content of each station, materials, tools, etc.

5. Design the lines/cells layout so that products flow

6. Adapt or create a daily scheduling function to support the lines/cells needs

7. Train, train and train again

their different variations. In other cases, it may be more practical to set up two or more lines that can be run at the same time. One line will typically accommodate products that are fairly standard. The others will be for products that may be unique or vary widely from the norm. The latter may have longer takt times, or be able to accommodate those products that require extra steps.

Whatever the case may be, the objective is to make value-added activities flow, and to the full extent possible, for them to flow with balance — which means each workstation should take approximately the same amount of time. But the concept of balance must be expanded from how it may have been perceived in the past. Instead of balance being applied solely to an individual product, a basic need is to achieve balance throughout the entire production process. The whole operation, all the products to be assembled on a given day, and the resources required — both human and mechanical — need to be taken into consideration. Depending on the size of the company and the complexity of the products it produces, balance and flow may only be achieved with the help of scheduling software developed for this task.

Seasonal Environments

A review of sales data for the past few years will determine if sales fluctuate throughout the year with some kind of predictable seasonality. If this is the case, it may not be practical or economically prudent to increase capacity to meet projected seasonal peaks. Since demand at certain times may outstrip a company's ability to supply, a disconnect may be necessary between the time the company will deliver products and the time the products will be made. In such cases, production leveling may be prudent. Rather than

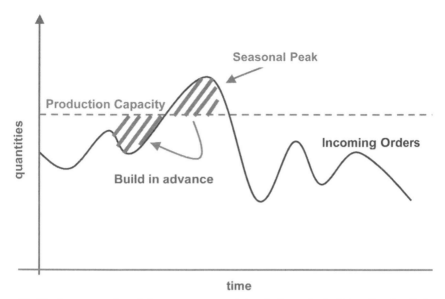

Fig. 5 - In seasonal environments, some of the peak can be built in advance -
up to the point of customization

establishing production capacity at the maximum level, it
usually makes more sense for capacity to fall between maximum and minimum anticipated demand because in most
cases it's easier to expand capacity than to cut it back.

If this strategy is employed, it may make sense for the
company to build some inventory in advance of anticipated
seasonal peaks in order to have stock available when capacity is constrained. These will usually be standard, off-the-
shelf items, or units completed only to the point that customization begins to occur. Then, in high months, standard
products will for the most part be delivered out of inventory and production capacity will be devoted largely to keeping up with custom-product demand.

Therc are several additional ways to deal with seasonal peaks in demand:

1. A second or eventually third shift may be added.

2. Seasonal workers may be brought on to handle some activities. If what would normally be excess equipment is available, this may be put to use.

3. There may be an opportunity to out source some activities to local third party subcontractors. If this is the case, it may make sense to provide some work to these subcontractors during the low season so that they have the required capacity available for the company during the high season. This requires a careful assessment of the specific situation as it may complicate the handling of excess personnel during the valleys. The achievement of a careful balance can be obtained over time as market demand grows and the company positions itself to meet the changing market demands.

4. As mentioned above, another possibility could be to produce a quantity of standard products or subassemblies to the point at which the first level of customization would normally begin. These might be stored and brought out for customization during the high season. While this approach may not always be feasible, a variation of this strategy usually will work.

Customizing from stock tends to be slightly more expensive than building from scratch, but in a highly seasonal market, no other alternative may exist. If some product indeed is to be made ahead of anticipated demand, important implications may be raised concerning the use of resources and the availability of materials and components. This means a forecast for the manufacturing of these items will be required and a process should be developed to determine when and under what circumstances these products are to be taken out of stock in order to supply customer needs.

Sales Is Responsible for Forecasting

Who should make the forecast? Sales should do so because sales works day in and day out with customers and is responsible for implementing the company's marketing strategies. We have often seen that the sales organization is reluctant to take on this responsibility. Nevertheless, because the Sales department is closest to the market and to customers, it is this department that possesses the knowledge necessary to perform the task. Admittedly, the first attempts may not be as accurate as everyone would like, but as time passes sales will become more adept and the accuracy of forecasts the group produces will grow.

It's important to mention that while forecasts are never accurate, as time goes by the information provided will allow an important transformation to take place. In the first place, forecasting makes possible the purchase of long lead materials and components and this can improve market performance in terms of meeting the dates customers want products delivered. Over time, sales personnel should become more aware of supply chain issues the sales department can help alleviate through accurate forecasting.

Second, sales are not managed by objective in many organizations. Forecasting will provide the sales department with an opportunity to review results on a regular basis so that corrective action can be taken as required.

Forecast information will be used by scheduling to plan capacity requirements, and it will be used by sourcing for ordering materials and components. Materials availability is an important key to meeting customer want dates. Whatever cannot be purchased and delivered in time for the company to produce a product when a customer places an order will need to be ordered far enough in advance to be on hand when needed. This is one reason why it's important for forecasts to be broken out into product type or category. Particular attention needs to be paid to those products that require special or long-lead parts or materials. Forecasts will allow what will be needed to be determined well in advance so that orders can be placed.

Another reason historical data should be grouped in a logical way — perhaps by product category or type or by the options each contains — is so the facility can be designed to accommodate right product mix. Sales should collaborate and be a part of the Lean team and assist in the review of information for the last few years as well as the last few months. As already mentioned, this analysis should include an effort to determine seasonal fluctuations.

The needs and the desires of the market can change, of course, so it's also important to assess market trends. Trend information typically comes from competitors through customers and from industry trade associations and journals. In addition, the company may have certain objectives or be following a strategic direction that will lead to faster growth in certain areas. This should be factored in, and the facility designed accordingly with care given to designing in flexibility in output capabilities.

Laying Out the Lines

In order to create maximum production efficiency, how to flow and schedule products in a way that minimizes unproductive time must be determined. Therefore, an important part of the Lean Transformation requires the determination of the best layout for the factory floor, taking into account workflow and the space requirements of material supply. This can be a complicated and time-consuming task. One of our clients, for example, has a universe of 90 machines within the manufacturing facility. Depending on what product a customer purchases, only 20 of these machines might be used. Another configuration might require 30, another 40, and so on. Some configurations will use the same number of machines but in a different work sequence. Typical lot sizes for these products are in the neighborhood of 50 units.

To determine how to lay out the plant for flow in this particular case, we first separated the different product variations into types and established a basic routing for each

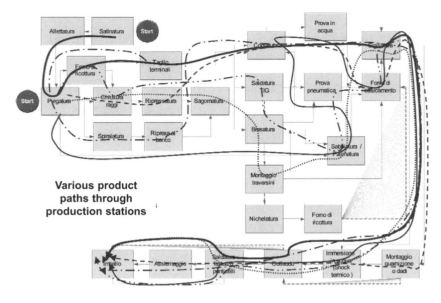

Various product
paths through
production stations

Fig. 6 — Flow of different products through the stations of the shop floor

type. We then looked for a way to arrange the machines that would require the shortest distance to be traveled and the smallest number of loopbacks for each product type. This would provide the best layout and optimum placement of machines.

When drawing the layout of a line or cell, it's important to build in flexibility so that changes are easy to make when the time comes to shift from one product to another.

We've found it's best to start with macro-mapping. Divide the process into basic process blocks. These may consist of several machines that are used in combination. Place them on a drawing in a logical sequence. Then take the different product families and determine which basic blocks they will flow through and the route they will follow through these process blocks. We call this the macro "spaghetti" chart.

Once a path line is drawn for each product (through the basic blocks it goes through), production lines can be super-imposed one on top of another in order to see where the routing is the same and where it is different. The goal is to develop a concept layout so that the basic processes are organized in a manner that will satisfy the production needs of most of the products with as few loop backs as possible. By approaching the task in this way, a graphical picture can be developed showing the best layout for the variety and combination of products to be manufactured. This is a way of visualizing the opportunities for layout design. At this stage, measurements taken to determine the actual, value-added process will be limited. Only after analyzing products within various families will the most effective macro layout be determined.

Manufacturing loopbacks are not desirable, of course, but sometimes they are unavoidable in a complex environment with low volume production. This does not mean that Lean principles are not being applied, but rather that they are applied in a way that takes into account the conditions a specific environment presents, including products to be manufactured, a product's variability, different cycle times and available capital equipment.

Once a concept layout has been developed that organizes process blocks so that most of the products can be satisfied, major blocks can be analyzed in greater detail. Each may include a number of machines or fixtures and these in turn may provide alternative routing for some products, eliminating more loopbacks.

A question that sometimes arises is how to balance the opportunity to have dedicated lines with the flexibility needed to support short volume, highly variable environments. Every case is different and it is not wise to set a rule for it. The analysis of the specific applications   determines the amount of capital investment required to meet the needs of these applications, while at the same time retaining flexibility and minimizing the total investment.

Another aspect to consider is that in highly variable environments, it may be impossible to balance (and measure) the myriad of products being produced. For example, we have a customer that has several product lines. One has four families, and within each the various models' cycle times differ by more than 80%. These product lines have more than 3,500 different codes. As a result, it is virtually impossible to measure and balance each and every product. Does this mean that Lean cannot be applied? Certainly not. A macro layout can be done enabling the flow of value added activities. In cases such as this, it is also important that operators and line leaders learn how to balance their own work, as the different products are made available for manufacturing.

Takt Time

An important concept in continuous flow manufacturing is what is known as "takt time" by Lean producers. "Takt" is a German word indicating the rhythm of a musical score. In Lean Production, it is the rate of sales in the marketplace, the drum beat of consumption. This is the beat to which to adjust the pace of a manufacturing operation — except in rare cases when this is impractical due to a highly seasonal environment as previously discussed. The goal is to have raw materials, or parts and components from suppliers, enter one door and flow with hardly a pause as they are assembled into finished goods. These in turn should move out another door, onto the loading dock and into trucks that deliver them to customers.

It may be helpful to imagine your suppliers as tributaries that flow into a river, which is your assembly operation. The tributaries and the river flow at the speed of sales and pro-

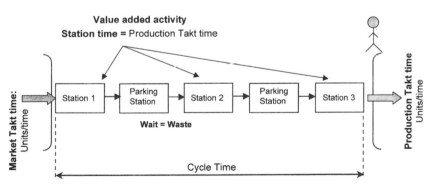

Market Takt time = Rate at which the market needs the product (demand rate)
Production Takt time = Rate at which a final product crosses the finish line which needs to match market takt time

Fig. 7 — Market takt time and production takt time

duction, or takt time. This is the pace you want those for-merly high speed machines to run, and the pace your assembly operators need to work. As you convert to continuous flow, you will probably identify logjams in some areas and rapids in others that need to be adjusted so that everything comes into balance. To "balance" a line, you may need to add workers to speed up passage through the jams. You might add tasks to workers in order to slow down the pace in areas requiring less time. The objective is to have the line move at a constant speed from one end to the other. Our experience has been that balancing a line can always be achieved either by taking into account the particular product or the mix of products to be made during a certain day.

Takt Times in Highly Variable Situations

When customers order customized products, it's often the case that many variations will be created from a basic platform. Some units will require production steps that others do not. Since Lean Production calls for continuous and balanced work flow, this creates a scheduling challenge. If a single assembly line is used, a product that requires extra steps will hold up other products, since not every unit moving through will be required to stop at each workstation. We have, for example, one client that manufactures a product for which one subassembly — that may or may not be required — takes seven hours to complete. The same unit has another optional subassembly that requires 25 hours. Some units require both subassemblies, and others only one or the other. Still others may require neither. Imagine the wasted manpower and plant utilization if the entire line were to be held up for 25 hours because of a unit that needed that particular subassembly.

This can be mitigated by creating different routings that send products requiring extra steps along alternative paths. At times a unit may rejoin the main line. This might be compared to scheduling local trains that stop at every station and express trains that run from one large city to another. At times the local train will need to get off the main line onto a side track so the express doesn't have to slow down and wait.

The layout and design of the production lines will depend on the volumes the sales organization believes it will sell. Nevertheless, in almost all cases when parallel lines are planned, flexibility should be built in because of the possibility of changes in the market or of other unforeseen circumstances. As mentioned, one line may be intended to produce more standard products — those requiring approximately the same number of steps and the same amount of time — and another line may be set for more complex products with highly variable takt times. Even so, the best solution will be for both lines to be laid out in a manner that makes it possible for them to be easily adapted and set up to run either kind of product should the need arise. In some cases, the fact that certain activities require personnel with specific skills must be taken into account. If the required skills can be taught to existing personnel, then the solution is to increase the knowledge level of those already associated with the process. But sometimes this may not be possible. An example might be a hospital where a need exists to have specific nursing skills that require a particular type of nursing degree. A limited amount of work may be available for these types of skilled personnel, but nonetheless, the need exists to have them. In such a situation, consideration must be given to developing a layout that enables the optimal use of these resources.

Balancing Lines

Takt time and the time required at each workstation need to be considered. In order to balance a line, a detailed time study of the complete process ought to be undertaken. It's best to use actual times and to avoid the use of "standard" times. (The process is depicted graphically in Fig. 8)

An activity to be measured should be conducted with people from the actual line because they can help by explaining why things are done in a certain way. The balancing process should include the following activities:

• Measure each and every activity performed during the process selected;

• Every activity measured needs to be evaluated in order to separate value-added activities from non value-added ones;

• Non value-added activities need to be eliminated, or reduced to the minimum or assigned to an external person

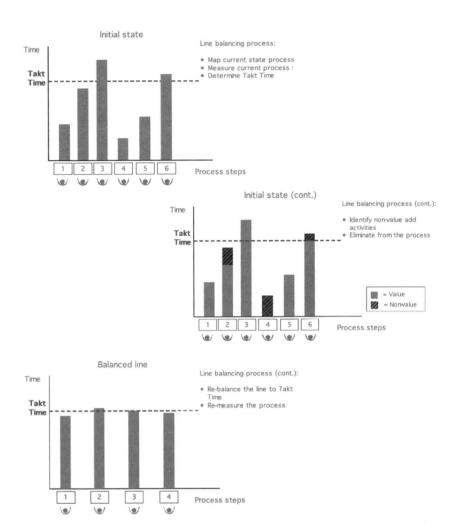

Fig. 8 - Example of balancing analysis; the first step is to measure each activity as it is; the second is to separate value-adding activities from non value-adding; last is to redesign the line in order to distribute value-adding activities among the stations and to eliminate non value-adding activities.

so that people in the main process perform only value-added activities. Some activities, even if they are not adding value, should not be eliminated at the first iteration. This will be held for a future process improvement session.

• Value-added activities should be distributed to each position of the line in an effort to reach a leveled distribution of time;

• It needs to be verified that the workstation can be designed with the assigned activities. For example, can material be distributed ergonomically? Can one person handle the number of machines assigned? If not, the balancing needs to be reworked until a feasible solution is reached.

Workstation Takt Times Need to Be Balanced

In order to balance a line, the longest takt time required by a workstation needs to be equal to or an even multiple of the other workstations. For example, if the longest workstation takt time in a line is six minutes, the others need to be the same or three or two minutes. For the line to be in balance, two of the three-minute operations or three of the two-minute operations should be scheduled in a way that balances out this six minute operation.

When individual products are being customized, some operations or installation of subassemblies may take an inordinate amount of time and could hopelessly throw off takt and hold up production of other items if not dealt with in some way. Therefore, as mentioned above, it may be advisable to establish side tracks or parking stations where some products may be stored or where time-consuming work may be performed while products not requiring this step move past them. This is one way the variability in takt time for different products can be accommodated.

Balancing a line may not be an easy job. One of our clients builds a textile product that is characterized by a number of small steps of different durations. A universe of machines is required that may be set up differently along the process, using different thread colors, for example. Some of the activities use up very little takt time. This is not an issue as long as more than one activity can be assigned to the same workstation. But some last longer than the takt time, making the design of the line extremely tricky. (See Fig 9, below)

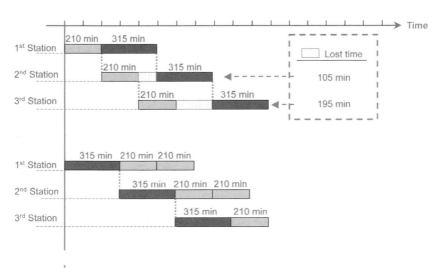

Fig. 9 — Optimal scheduling sequence when products with different takt times are run through the same line

Many Factors Must Be Considered

We have come to the conclusion that balancing and designing such a layout is an art. Some of the factors which must be taken into consideration include the size of various products moving through, material handling needs, and the alternative routes which may be taken due to the various customization activities necessary for certain products. There are no specific rules to follow. What must be kept in mind at all times are the objectives, which are: to minimize distances products and materials will have to travel, to minimize and/or eliminate non value-added activities, to make value added activities flow in a manner that is closest to balanced, to minimize the distances that need to be covered by workers involved in adding value, to assure flow, as much as possible, and to optimize people (rather than machine) utilization. The closer we are to meeting these objectives, the more efficient the overall process will be.

Workstation Design Considerations

When designing a layout, special considerations need to be given to each workstation, specifically:

• Ergonomic: after a Lean Transformation each person normally produces 30-50% to 100% more than before. The work area should be designed to eliminate the possibility of injuries due to repetitive strain injuries (RSI). The ability to adjust the station to accommodate persons of different heights is one example.

• Tools: The kinds of tools and their availability to the operator should be evaluated with the increased productivity each person has to reach in mind. Some tools may no longer be suitable. For example, lighter drills may replace heavier ones. In some cases, it might make sense to rethink the product itself in order to make assembly easier. For example, it may make sense to move screws so that the product can be assembled vertically rather than horizontally because it is easier to use a screwdriver that hangs vertically from above. Another possibility, if applicable, is to use a 90° screwdriver. Tools should be arranged so that they are easy to reach and to use. They might hang from above or be placed next to the area of use on properly designed supports.

• The transfer of product along the process: It should be possible for the product to proceed with minimum effort and to be manipulated by the operators without them having to lift it.

• Materials arrangement: Materials should be distributed in ways that are easily accessible by the operators. Also, materials manipulation should not create stress on muscles as could be the case when located above the shoulder or behind the work position. Requiring the operator to rotate frequently should be avoided.

• Material distribution: Materials should be provided to the workstation in a way that does not interrupt the operator. If possible, double manipulations should be avoided. For example, packing standards ought to be defined with suppliers to make them suitable to proceed directly to the workstation. If models are changed on the line, i.e., the line must shift from one product to another, it should be possible for this to happen within one takt time. This means the line will lose only one piece per changeover.

Many approaches exist to minimizing changeover time, which are particularly appropriate for small lot sizes and frequent changeovers. In some cases, a complete set up can be done from behind the workstations by loading materials into bins and rotating the bins' support 180 degrees once the change over is to take place. In this case, the changeover time is practically nonexistent. In other cases there may be a need to kit certain materials and components. This is particularly true when the lots are small and parts and components are large.

• Standardized work instructions: Work sequences should be clearly established and indicated at each workstation together with the time allowed for each model.

Moving from Conceptual Layout to Factory Floor

A conceptual layout is only the first step. It is developed based on the objective of achieving flow. Before it is implemented, however, it needs to be worked out on the actual factory space. Such things as the position of columns or other major physical objects or obstacles that cannot be moved must be taken into account. It's almost inevitable that a conceptual layout will have to be modified or adjusted when translated to an actual factory floor.

Other Layout Issues

The location of hoists and their availability often must be dealt with. Time spent waiting for a hoist to become available is wasted. In one factory we designed, before we began the transformation, two out of nine hours were wasted every day because workers had to wait to use a hoist. Depending on where the hoist was positioned, everyone in a line would remain idle because the line couldn't move and no work could be done until the hoist became available. Obviously, thought must be given to how such a situation might be avoided. Often an alternative can be found such as using a manual boom instead of a hoist, which is how we opened up this particular bottleneck.

Working out the optimal layout can take some time. How much time and effort will be required will vary, of course, depending on the product to be manufactured. Some designs are by nature more complicated than others and offer more alternative possibilities. In our experience, it can take anywhere from one to six weeks to develop a layout that takes everything into consideration.

Multiple Lines

As noted, in some cases it may be helpful to have lines dedicated to building fairly simple products and some devoted to more complex ones. In this way, the highly variable products can be run without upsetting the flow of the more standard variety.

In one case we created two production lines for a client that makes a large product. One line was for products that fall into what might be called a standard type, and the other for more complicated and varied assemblies. Even in the so-called standard line, however, a great deal of variation can be handled. For this to be done in the most efficient way, we tried to minimize the number of places along the line where these variations occur. These can be viewed as the side tracks, or stations, mentioned above. There are products that need to move onto these side tracks to have the variations taken care of while others that can move along faster pass by on a different track. The workers who man the workstations where the complicated or varied assembles are completed must be multi-skilled so that they can perform whatever special or unusual tasks are called for. Usually, a set group of people man these stations, but from time to time more manpower may be required. In the case of one client, what we call "floaters" are called on to help when needed. These floaters move around and perform different jobs throughout the plant.

Cost, fixtures, equipment, available space, volumes to be produced and so forth are all parts of the mix to be considered in how lines are laid out or whether multiple lines are an option. If space and equipment are available, having additional lines that are not always manned can be beneficial because this will mean no time is lost during set up. The line not in use can be made ready, and the appropriate materials put in position while the first is still in use. Operators can then move one by one, station by station in a progressive transfer, from the first line to the next as each one's designated activities are completed. In this manner, time will be saved that would otherwise be lost while waiting for a run to be finished.

In these cases, consideration needs to be given to the lot sizes to be produced. It is not desirable to have operators moving continually from one line to another. This can be disruptive and it can also create morale issues.

Material Handling Considerations

Movement and location of materials is also an issue to be carefully considered. If lot sizes are small, 1-50 for example, it may be necessary to change materials quite often. If the materials are small in size, this should not be a problem. Such material can be positioned at the workstation site. But in cases where materials are large or arrive on pallets that are difficult to handle, it may take some thought to work out the best solution.

Materials distribution can be critical especially in the case of frequent model changes and small lot sizes. Different solutions might be as follows:

• Bring one or more pallets with all materials required for each model, if volume for a product is large enough;

• Prepare dedicated kits that can be divided by production order and by model, by group of orders, or by slot of time. (Example: one kit can provide one hour of work.) This is especially effective for bulky components and small lot sizes (1 to 20 pieces).

If a workable strategy cannot be determined, a material handler may not have time to physically change materials, or there may not be enough space to accommodate material for more than one product. Depending on quantity and the size of the components for each model, as well as production lot size and takt time, it may be necessary to redesign the central warehouse in order to make it possible for forklift operators to replenish the line as required. This issue is often ignored with the result that material handlers must constantly surf the warehouse to find required materials. The impact of this can be quite negative because more material handlers may be required than might otherwise be needed. Alternatively, it could happen that line stoppages may become commonplace because handlers do not have time to make the necessary materials/components changes.

For an operation to run smoothly, material handlers must have detailed knowledge of the production process, including the sequence of assembly, and provide specific materials when they are needed. Changeover and delivery need to occur on time without the creation of traffic issues.

Material handling also has implications for scheduling and this will be dealt with in the chapter devoted to that subject.

Takt Time Should Even Out Over Time

In a highly complex manufacturing environment, some products may take two or three times the takt time to produce as others. The goal is for market takt time and production takt time to equal out over a period of time such as a day, a few days or a week. But on a particular day this may not be the case because of the complexity of products moving through. Suppose, for example, the takt time of movement through a facility is 200 minutes. In other words, every 200 minutes a finished product should come off the end of the line. What happens when a particular subassembly for a custom job takes 500 minutes? Obviously, everything else should not be held up, waiting for this subassembly to be completed. Instead, the most efficient way must be determined for that particular product to be scheduled and to move through production and assembly. This will probably mean the 500-minutes subassembly will have to be initiated 300 minutes ahead of the time the unit that will require it enters production. To get a mental picture of this, you might think of a cook who wants to have dinner ready at eight o'clock in the evening. The roast may take three hours to cook and the rice twenty minutes. So the cook will begin the roast at five o'clock and the rice at twenty to eight.

Timing Is Critical

The timing of the start of each subassembly needs to be such that all of them will be completed at the right times — the times when they will be needed in final assembly. As in the case of the cook mentioned above, the strategy usually will be to begin the subassemblies up front so they all are ready when needed. But what happens when the meal plan calls for roast beef, which takes three hours, and roast duck, which takes only an hour, but there is only one roaster? Suppose the cook cannot afford another roaster, or if he could, he wouldn't have room for it? There's no way to have them both completed simultaneously. Increasing manpower and resources may be impossible or difficult in the short term. Of course, in some cases, subcontractors may be called upon to help out in a crunch, or it may be possible to rent machines in order to increase capacity. But if none of these measures will solve an issue, some subassemblies — the roast above for example — might have to be started even further ahead — four hours in this case — so that the roaster will be freed up in time to cook the duck.

In addition to this, there is the issue of having the right type and quantity of the right materials when needed. In the case of purchased items, forecasting can be used to determine ahead of time what will be required so that hiccups will be held to a minimum. In the case of components and subassemblies built in house or by subcontractors, attention must be paid to their timely completion.

Creating Supermarket Buffers

In the case of small products it may be possible to create buffers of components or materials. Then, if a part doesn't arrive when it should or the equipment in that "tributary" doesn't allow it to be made fast enough, the final assembly line will not be held up. But if the subassemblies are very large, such as those for airplanes, trucks, trailers, commercial refrigeration units or other large products, a buffer of sub components may not be possible. No place may be available, for example, to store airplane wings or trailer or truck sides which could easily be 50+ feet long. Nevertheless, when a buffer is possible, creating one can be an efficient way to mitigate the situations discussed above.

Buffers should have a design criterion that is strict and clear:

• Quantity has to be sufficient to keep things flowing so that subsequent stations are not required to stop and wait.

• The produced subassembly quantity should be used up over a specified period of time such as one day, one shift, or a few hours.

• Minimum space should be taken up by the buffer.

• It should be determined which makes more sense, having the extra components or subassemblies in a buffer, or an investment in an additional line to produce them so that a buffer isn't needed.

• Scheduling should have the capacity and ability to establish what to build and store in the buffers.

• Buffers need to expand and shrink like an accordion reaching zero or near zero at times during the day.

Flexibility of Due Dates
As already has been touched upon, scheduling is critical

to the efficient functioning of highly variable manufacturing environments. The task of scheduling begins at the time the Master Production Schedule (MPS) is built. It's paramount that the MPS not be determined by sales representatives or the sales team, but rather by the ability of the production environment to produce products at the required times. This means a sales order and delivery date should only be confirmed after production has reviewed and verified the order can be fulfilled within the requested timeframe. What can be considered feasible depends not only on the availability of materials and components, but also on the total mix of products to be scheduled coupled with the manufacturing plant capacity both in terms of equipment as well as human resources. There is almost always a limit to what can be accomplished within a given amount of time.

Flexing to Arrive at a Slower Takt Time

Let's say an assembly line is designed to produce 120 units per hour, and customer demand falls to 75 per hour. What should be done? Assuming the demand slowdown will continue for more than a week or so, in order to avoid building inventory, it's best to slow the rate of production to match customer demand. This will usually mean using the same equipment, but with fewer operators. For example, it might make sense to deploy seven workers instead of ten, and have these seven "flex" to cover what would be manned workstations in a full-capacity situation. In other words, the

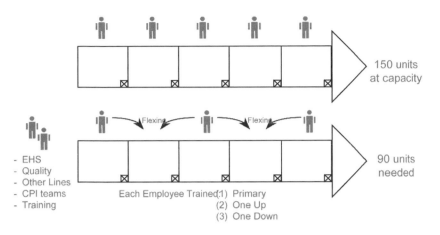

Fig. 10 — Flexing between stations in order to meet market demand

workers will now move between machines, performing an operation on one and then moving to another. In other cases, flexing may mean having fewer workers perform more assembly tasks in a given workstation, thus increasing the time a unit will remain in it.

Due to equipment and process considerations, a finite number of throughput volumes exist that allow for a balanced line. It's important to understand this in order to be prepared for situations such as when an operator is absent for the day and no replacement is available. It may be impossible to balance a line with one less worker. To avoid the disruption that would result from timing being thrown off, the next takt time level down should be determined that permits a balanced operation. It's common for a chart to be developed that shows the line volumes that support a balanced operation, and the number of operators required for each one.

67

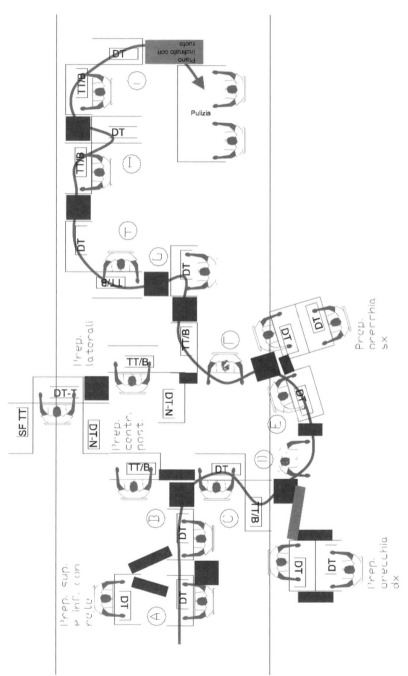

Fig. 11 — Line configuration for 432 pcs/hour

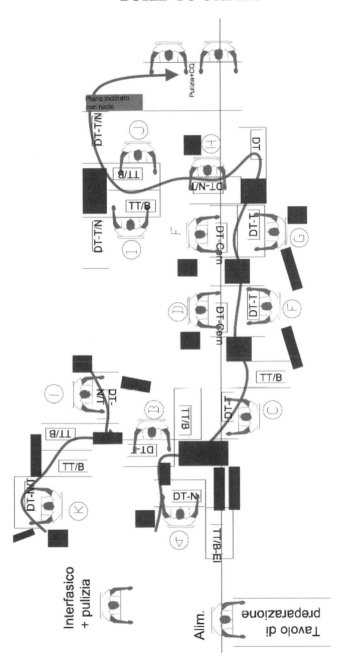

Fig. 12 — Line configuration for 304 pcs/hour

What should be done with the excess operators when the operation has "flexed down?" They can support other teams, undergo training to educate them on operations or procedures that may be new to them, work on an ongoing quality issues, become active in other Lean initiatives or perform 5S activities.

Flowing People Not Products

Of course, not all products flow. Some, like a house, a large and heavy machine such as a ship engine, a commercial refrigeration unit or a blow molding machine may remain in the same location while being assembled. It may be possible

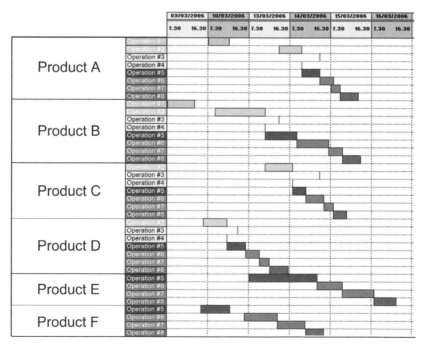

Fig. 13 — Example of of Gantt chart with building activities sequence

to move such things but this can be a very costly proposition. In such cases, it's workers who flow in a balanced way as the product (house, ship engine or whatever) grows toward completion.

When the people are what moves from one location to another, it is nonetheless important to create a sense of flow. Otherwise problems can occur that would probably not happen in an assembly line situation.

Creating a sense of flow in these situations isn't always easy but there are several ways it can be done. Our experience has been that it's best to do so using visuals rather than words or numbers. As was mentioned in the section earlier on visual management, visual tools allow workers to "see" what kind of progress has been made and which tasks have been accomplished. As you recall, we mentioned the example of a United Way fund-raising chart in a town square in which a thermometer is colored red as funds are raised toward a goal. A Gantt chart (http://www.ganttchart.com) showing the various production phases for the machine will usually work. In this way, everyone can see in real time the progress that's being made.

The most common problems occur as a result of proper materials not being available when needed. A crew may go to work on a particular job, run out of what they need and have to stop. This can cause a problem because certain work may have to be completed before the next step can logically be taken. The same can be true whether a product is flowing on

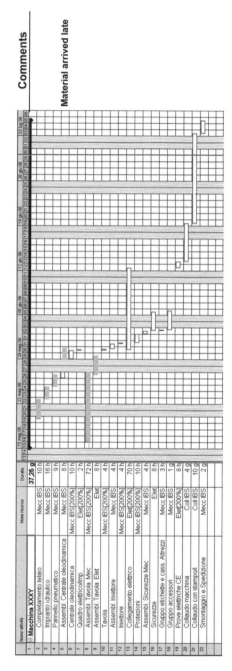

Fig. 14 — Example of Gantt chart with building activities sequence updated by operators

□ = an empty box indicates the length in time of the specific activity

▓ = green fill indicates the time already spent of the specific activity

a line or stationary. The wallboard should not go up before the wiring goes in, and the walls cannot be painted until the wallboard goes up. The point is, it may not be possible to change the order of work flow. So when the painters arrive they will not be able to do their job. This can cause a domino effect, hopelessly throwing off the product schedule.

There are other cases, however, when it is not obvious that work hasn't been completed that needs to be done before the next step is taken. This is why the visual flow chart is necessary. Otherwise, when the next crew arrives, they may or may not see that the crew before them didn't finish. As a result, they may go ahead and perform work that later will have to be undone or the product may have quality problems.

We had a client, for example, that builds refrigeration banks. A compressor was missing on one job but the construction crew built the refrigeration bank anyway. When the compressor arrived, the workers had to disassemble what they had built in order to install the compressor. The head of production, however, comforted himself and others in the knowledge that his "workers were always busy." Too bad rework is an extremely unproductive way to keep them occupied.

Often in these environments when a work crew runs out of materials it will begin to cannibalize those designated for another phase of the project or product. When they complete what they have to do, what's needed for the next stage of assembly or construction may no longer be available.

Counterproductive work such as this can be avoided by creating a sense of flow that allows everyone to see and know what's taking place. Often we do this with colors. The activities that need to take place are laid out in sequential order on a big chart. When an activity is completed, it is colored in. When something has not been colored in, it hasn't been completed. When the next crew arrives, this tells them they should not begin the activity they've been assigned until the previous one is completed.

Managing Multi-Skilled Workers

It should be apparent from the foregoing discussion that workers in a highly variable environment often need to be multi-skilled. They need to be able to move from one workstation or job to another without missing a beat. What's the best way to manage workers such as these? They need to be allotted the right amount of time to do a job, they need to have the right skills to do it, and they must have the right materials available when needed. In addition, these individuals must be capable of a certain amount of self-management. They need to be able to make decisions on what needs to be done, and they also must work within jointly established, predefined boundaries. Additionally, their time ought to be scheduled when workflow and specific jobs are being scheduled through the plant. Highly skilled workers are an important key to success and are usualy justifiably proud of the work they do. Typically they like to do things "their own way." Winning them over and getting their buy-in is a critical factor to a successful transformation. For this reason, the Lean transformation needs to be carefully thought through and carried out with this in mind.

Managers Must Transform into Coaches

In a transformation from an autocratic environment to a participative one, a need exists for a leader who understands the role he or she needs to play and can allocate resources with a minimum of friction. As time passes, this person needs to evolve into a coach or advisor and the workers should more and more be given the latitude to manage themselves. This goal should be understood by everyone at the outset. More will be said on this later.

Scheduling and People

A highly variable environment raises deployment issues that a repetitive environment does not. The correct skill sets will be needed at specific points in time. Appropriate management and scheduling are required to allocate and assign the people with the right skill sets. As already noted, materials and tools need to be in the right places when they are needed. As a result, each workstation should have a schedule of what will be occurring during the day. This ought to communicate who will be doing what and when they will be doing it.

Material handling needs to have this schedule and to use

it to make sure the right tools, fixtures, and materials are there and ready at the appropriate times. In some operations the people who do this are called facilitators. They are always working ahead and aware of the upcoming production schedule so that when product moves from one station to the next, everything is ready for work to begin. It should not be the job of the station operators to perform this function. If it is, large amounts of time will be lost as the operators take the time needed to search out and gather up the materials and tools needed to do a job. This will be dealt with in more depth in the next chapter.

Recap

In designing a Lean manufacturing facility it's essential to establish plant capacities and a layout that will facilitate the matching of production takt times with the pace of marketplace consumption. This will require a realistic projection based on what has occurred in the past, where the market appears to be headed and the company's strategic objectives. Sales should play a key role in developing this since the sales team is closest to customers and the market.

In highly seasonal environments it doesn't always make sense to build capacity to meet peaks levels since it is almost always easier to increase capacity than to cut it back. It normally makes more sense for capacity to fall between the maximum and minimum anticipated demand. To be able to accommodate peaks, it may make sense to build some inventory in advance of them. Usually, this will be standard, off-the-shelf items or units completed only to the point that customization can begin to occur. Other strategies include bringing in seasonal help and subcontracting some work during peak times.

In determining the best layout for the factory floor, we usually start by separating the different product variations into types and establishing a basic routing for each. Machines might be grouped into basic process blocks (several machines normally used in combination). To find the best placement, an arrangement should be sought that will require the shortest distance to be traveled and the smallest number of loopbacks.

Once this has been done, a path can be drawn for each product variation. These drawings can be superimposed on one another to see where the routings are the same and where they are different. The goal is to develop a conceptual layout. Once the best conceptual layout has been determined it will have to be translated to the actual factory floor and will almost always require modification due to physical objects that cannot be moved such as columns, as well as to take into account the needs of material handling and storage.

It's often the case that many product variations will be created from a basic platform. Some will require steps that others do not. It may make sense, therefore, to create different routings that send products along alternative paths as is done with railroad trains. Express trains (those products requiring fewer steps) can then pass by locals that stop at every station (highly customized variations). It may also make sense to create two lines: One for more standard products and another for more customized versions. In any event, maximum flexibility should be built in since the market may change.

In order to balance a line, the longest takt time required by a workstation needs to be a multiple of the other stations. Operations can then be arranged so that products move along in lock step and no operators are left idle, waiting for a product to appear.

If not enough workers are available to man each workstation or if the takt time needs to be lowered due to a reduction in the marketplace takt time, it will be necessary to flex down by redistributing operations among workers in a way that balances the line. This means fewer workers will be required because each one of them will perform more operations.

In a Lean operation each worker will, on average, produce more than they did in the non-Lean work environment, so workstations should be designed ergonomically to eliminate stress that could cause injury. In addition, work should be standardized and the right tools and materials need to be available when needed. This is usually handled by facilitators. A number of considerations were covered for material handling including the "kitting" of components in advance and supermarket buffers that hold components or parts that cannot be made fast enough to keep up with takt time. In addition, products should move from one station to the next with minimum effort on the part of operators.

Subassemblies must also be available when needed and this means work must begin far enough in advance for this to happen. (A comparison was made to a chef who needs to start cooking items at different times so that they are all ready for dinner at the same time.)

In the case of large assemblies that are stationary, a sense of flow can be created by using a Gantt chart. This can also communicate what operations have been performed so that work will not be undertaken that should not happen until requisite steps are taken.

For a Lean operation to function as efficiently as possible, workers must make decisions and be capable of a certain amount of self-management. Leaders must understand this and work toward becoming coaches or advisors rather than remaining in the role of authoritarian bosses.

Chapter Three: Scheduling and Support

Each day can be quite different in a highly variable, complex-assembly environment. Different lines and different machines may be used. Some may sit idle all day, depending on the product mix du jour. As already noted, people who work in this environment need to be multi-skilled and able to move easily from one task to another. Someone — the daily scheduler — has to schedule all of the shop floor activities and communicate the schedule to everyone involved so that each individual knows where he or she is supposed to be at any given time, and what he or she ought to be doing.

In Lean, build-to-order factories, final assembly is almost always accomplished by combining subassemblies. As discussed in the last chapter, the sequence in which major subassemblies are built may not be the same as that of final assembly due to the differing times required to build each subassembly. Scheduling is critical in order to maintain takt time and flow because the time needed to construct the various subassemblies may be vastly different. Some may take ten minutes, others ten hours. Bringing them all together at the right times for final assembly to continue at a pace that matches the drumbeat of the marketplace requires scheduling the construction of each as precisely as possible. Of course, this means it is not only necessary to develop a scheduling sequence for final assembly. All the activities that lead up to it have to be scheduled as well. This means not

BUILD TO ORDER

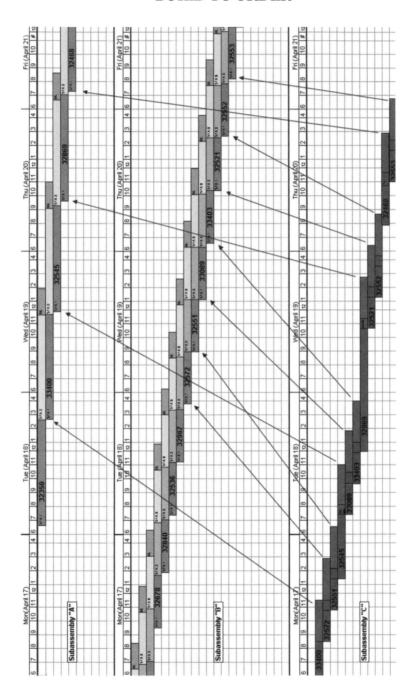

Fig. 15 — Scheduling Gant chart linking subassemblies to product build

82

only the construction of subassemblies but the procurement of components and raw materials. The daily scheduler's job is to perform these tasks, which means this individual occupies a central position at the heart of the organization. This function determines what will be produced, when it will be produced, who will perform each task, and at which station each task will be performed. The latter is specifically important in cases where a particular production phase can be done through various alternative routings within a plant.

It's not an overstatement to say that the job of the daily scheduler is critical.

Centralized Scheduling Is New For Most Plants

The need for daily scheduling invariably changes the way a manufacturing operation works. This function must manage production on a minute-to-minute basis. Typically, a universe of machines exists in a plant. The products to be produced on a given day need to pass through these machines and overload situations may easily develop. To avoid this it may sometimes be best for different machines to be used if an alternative routing is possible for a particular product. For example, if a product passes through machines A, B, and C, it may take ten minutes. But the same product may be able to pass through machines E, F, and G, which will produce the same result, but will take 30 minutes. Yet this may be the best solution for takt time, on-time delivery and flow to be maintained because it will mean a bottleneck can be avoided because of the machines needed and timing requirements of other products being routed through assembly on a given day.

In the past, supervisors were given a list of what needed to be done, sometimes once a week. They decided how the list would be produced through the lines, including the production sequence and the resources to be used. But without an understanding of the production sequences of other departments, and without the aid of scheduling software, the supervisor's determination may not have employed the most efficient production sequence and it may not have used resources with maximum efficiency. The supervisor may have scheduled work to maximize the efficiency within his department, but the result may not have coordinated as well as it might have with factors outside his purview. In addition, in the past synchronizing the various subassemblies was almost impossible in complex environments. As a result, quick meetings were often called and decisions made to rush a subassembly through the lines. This may have meant work had to come to a stop further along in the process. Operating in this way often resulted in significant inefficiencies, rushing, more changeovers than necessary, as well as the cannibalizing of products, materials and components. This is why it makes sense in the build-to-order Lean environment for the daily scheduler to let supervisors know what needs to be produced that day, the sequence in which this output needs to be produced, and what machines and people are needed to accomplish it. This is a dramatic change from the traditional way but it is absolutely necessary for the overall operation to perform at the highest level of efficiency.

Dealing with Unexpected Changes

What happens when unexpected changes occur in the production schedule? The supervisors need to consult with the scheduler who will work out a new plan to minimize the effect of the unexpected changes. Whenever a significant glitch happens, a domino effect often is created that causes a good deal of the day's work to be rearranged. The new schedule needs to be clearly communicated, discussed and understood by all who are affected. If delivery of a product will be delayed, customer service or sales will have to be informed. Shipping may already have been lined up so the person is in charge of freight will have to be notified, and so on.

Let's say a company builds trucks to order and there are two lines. One line builds two axle trucks and this is the standard product. This line has the capacity to build twelve of these per week. A second line is more specialized. Those with three axles or more are built here and more variability is possible. Let's say a certain configuration of orders needs to be delivered next week. For this to happen, a specified number of vehicles must move through. But next week, a job is coming up that will require an enormous amount of time because of its complexity. If the vehicle is not launched this week, on Wednesday for example, it cannot be completed on time. A complicating factor is that if it is launched then, the jig that was going to produce the other specials will no longer be available. Because we have built flexibility into the standard line, however, we are able to move special jobs to the standard line. Now, the sequence in which the specials and the standards moving through the standard line are scheduled will be critical so that the minimum amount of time will be lost. Let's say, for example, work at station A on a particular special takes twice as long as normal. The takt time will have been doubled so it will be twice as long before the truck at station A can move to station B. In addition to determining the best sequence — perhaps using scheduling software — the scheduler may also have the team at station B do its normal job and then move to another location to work there until the assembly at station A is complete.

The New Role of Supervisors

In the past, supervisors would have made the decisions concerning who would do a job, when it would be done and where it would be done. In a complex Lean environment, this can no longer be the case, which raises the question, what is the job of supervisors in this new setup?

The answer is simple. It is to make sure that what is produced is built to the established schedule. Supervisors must become leaders, coaches, mentors and trainers. They need to be ready to step in and help if someone is having trouble or to show them how to do a job. This means that supervisors need to know how to perform every job that may be required in his or her area of supervision. Currently, this may not be the case in some companies. Therefore, if supervisors come from outside the company, they will need to spend weeks actually building products in the area under their supervision. On the other hand, in cases where supervisors are promoted from within, it is absolutely necessary that they are taught the right skills and techniques to manage people. We've seen that supervisors are often chosen from inside the company and thrown into the job without training. In such situations, companies usually lose twice. They lose a good worker and they have someone in the new position who is most likely not prepared for or good at the job. Just because someone is a successful operator does not insure they will be a successful supervisor.

Often someone thrown into a supervisory position will take on the role of a mini dictator. For example, rather than consult with workers, explore alternatives and arrive at an agreement on what course to follow, they will skip what they may view simply as "niceties" and spout orders concerning what workers need to do. This may save a minute or two in the short run, but in the long run this way of operating is counterproductive. It prevents those under the supervisor from being part of a decision and thereby taking ownership of it. It also teaches these individuals not to think for them selves. Eventually they will become robots who rely completely on the boss to decide a course of action. This is not good for the operation, especially where workforce empowerment is a critical factor to success. For things to run smoothly, self-directed and self-correcting workers are what's needed. This is especially true in a highly complex environment. It is impossible for the boss to always be looking over everyone's shoulder. Things will work a lot better if people are able to think for themselves, make suggestions that are taken seriously, and in many cases decide on their own what needs to be done.

To reiterate, the new role of supervisors should be to help expedite, to maintain the rhythm of the line, to collect problems and suggestions and to call the appropriate support when needed such as quality, engineering or maintenance. Supervisors should also motivate workers. One way this is done is by involving them in coming up with solutions. This builds a team environment, mentality and spirit that can result in a highly productive environment. To reiterate, supervisors must be leaders, not dictators. They should do whatever they can to insure the goals for the day will be met, not so much by cracking a whip, but rather, by getting everyone to pull together.

What should a supervisor do when people finish a job early? This can happen when there is variability. Loading up another station with extra workers is not a good solution because this will likely create an imbalance. What would happen, for instance, if the workers start a job and don't have time to finish it? Plus, the takt time may be thrown off because extra workers got the job done faster. If this happens, even more people may be left standing around without anything to do. The result is that redistributing these workers along the line is likely to create more problems than it solves. As a rule, it should not be done. The best solution may be to have them clean up, put things in order, kit some materials, or perhaps learn a new skill. They can be assigned to a workstation they don't know to observe and learn.

In summary, it is the scheduler's job to insure the most efficient use of resources on a daily basis, and it is the job of supervisors to execute this schedule. Scheduling also needs to work closely with materials management in order to be always up to date on material arrivals and to let suppliers know possible production priorities changes. The scheduler needs to stay in touch with customer service or sales as well in order to let them know of scheduling changes and to stay on top of changes in priority that may be taking place in the market.

The Human Element

A word of caution may be appropriate. Moving people around from one task and work area (line, cell, workstation, et cetera) to another can appear to be chaotic and can cause morale to deteriorate if it is not handled properly. It's important for people to understand why changes are being made, i.e., why they are being moved and the logic behind these types of changes. This should be communicated in face-to-face meetings. A briefing ought to be held at the beginning of each day. Short meetings may also be required during the day to bring people up to speed when changes or hiccups cause the day's plan to be reworked. People need to feel a part of what's happening in order for them to perform at their highest capacity, and this means they have to be kept informed of the decisions that affect their work environment.

It's also important to keep teams together as a unit as much as possible. As time goes by, teams will form a cohesive unit. As they get more and more comfortable working together, performance accelerates. A disruption to the team can cause a drop in morale and a corresponding drop in performance. This is why it's important to preserve them as units and to let them control their own performance. Pressure from teammates to get a job done can be brutal. It can be an extremely productive tool in the pursuit of excellence and high performance.

Delivery Dates

As was mentioned earlier, calculating delivery dates can be tricky and should be done by scheduling. It should not be attempted by sales or customer service. The sequence of required delivery dates may not be the same sequence in which the items are produced. In a repetitive environment, the daily capacity for each product can be determined. This creates a certain number of "slots" per day or week. Once the slots for a day are filled, the scheduler is able to move to the next. But the task is not so simple in a complex and variable environment. What we have discovered when build-to-order products are moving through — some of which have subassemblies requiring many extra hours to complete — is that bottlenecks will be created. These bottlenecks will not always be in the same place. They may occur throughout the production process and be different at different times based on the mix of products being run — or perhaps more accurately, what the company is selling at a particular time.

High seasonality may dictate a change in production strategy to meet current or anticipated needs. Bottlenecks may be created not only by tied-up machines but by manning and subcontracting difficulties as well. Supply chain issues may be involved because what's needed in a custom environment may not always be in stock.

Often managers or sales personnel will estimate how long a job will take based on the total number of labor hours required but this can be misleading. If a product needs custom engineering, for example, time must be allowed for this to be accomplished. There is also the need to estimate how long a product will take to be produced. This is the case for engineered products built only on demand. In order to make this estimation, a basic drawing should be released and the production process identified. Of course, a job that requires ten hours of labor does not always take ten hours to complete. If ten people are put on it, for example, it might be possible to get it done in one hour. On the other hand, if parts or components that have a long lead time are called for and these are not in stock, the delivery date may have to move forward regardless of the amount of labor or hours required for assembly.

Prioritizing Orders

It may be important to consider where sales orders are coming from when determining the best way to manage them in order to maintain flow. If they are coming directly from customers, the company will of course want to fill them as quickly as possible. If an aftermarket order is received, the order usually ought to be dealt with immediately. Let's say your company makes some type of equipment, for example, and because of an accident or a breakdown the customer needs only a subassembly or some portion of a subassembly. What if the customer will be out of business until he has this part to replace the one that's broken? Because it's only one part of a whole machine, it will probably not take an entire cycle time. This can be very difficult to incorporate into the current daily schedule. But even so, it must be dealt with. A method or procedure should be established to handle cases such as this.

On the other hand, if orders are coming from a distribution center — whether internal or external — and an order is to replenish inventory, flexibility may exist that will allow scheduling the entire mix of products in the most efficient way.

Beware Making Promises on Delivery Dates

In highly variable environments, the scheduling function needs to work in partnership with sales. It should go without saying that the sales organization needs to have an idea or working framework of the time requirements for various products to keep in mind. Even so, the variables of a highly complex environment strongly suggest promises should not be made about delivery dates until the actual amount of time a custom job will take can be calculated and the delivery date confirmed by scheduling. The actual date will be based on engineering requirements, availability of parts and components, and the most efficient way to schedule the job through the facility in light of other jobs in the works that may require the same resources — for which firm due dates already exist. Obviously, rapport needs to exist between production scheduling and sales, and an information interface needs to be established and put in place.

It doesn't take much imagination to realize that misunderstandings and friction can easily come about, and this is why a healthy dialog is essential to the best interests of the company. To help this along, scheduling software allows for production simulations to be run as orders are received so that optimum timing for maximum efficiency can be determined.

Scheduling in Seasonal Environments

The strategy of building some inventory ahead of time to offset seasonal peaks was covered in the last chapter. Needless to say, having inventory on hand has scheduling implications. If stock items are available from inventory, it may be necessary to determine whether or not a sales order ought to be filled from stock — at least through the first stage of production. Naturally, the customization phase alone will take less time than building a complete product from scratch.

This approach can present an interesting dilemma. If product has been built to stock up to the point customization would normally begin, such platforms then are typically managed like an accordion. They are accumulated during the time of year when demand is lowest and depleted during the peak season. The challenge is to determine how best to manage this depletion so that inventory levels are as low as possible at the end of the peak season. At the same time, care needs to be taken that the company does not run out of products during the time when demand is still high and production volumes are straining resources. Data drivers are available for the scheduling software that will help in making a choice concerning whether to fill an order from stock or to build it from scratch. Factors that must be taken into consideration include the availability of materials and the ability to meet customer "want" delivery dates given current demand. When want dates become an issue, the alternatives need to be presented to sales and they should decide among them.

The Materials and Component Supply

Forecasting is important for a number of reasons. The

first, which was also discussed in the previous chapter, is to answer the need for projections in order to design and build a plant to handle anticipated demand. Second, a good forecast is needed to insure the right materials and components will be on hand when needed. This ought to be shared with suppliers so that they, too, can take the steps necessary to have materials available to supply your company's needs. This is particularly important now — the time in our history when this book is being written. The economies of China and India are growing rapidly and those in much of the rest of the world are booming. Scarcities of various materials and components are one result. Materials are bought when available so forecasting also helps suppliers plan ahead so they can have the material required to satisfy requests.

The demand for high customization along with competitive pressure creates a need for quick turnaround and delivery of complex products at competitive prices. This makes it important to have solid partnerships with suppliers. Companies that cannot rely on strong support from their supply chain may find themselves in difficult situations, particularly when they are not big enough to have much buying clout. When relatively small suppliers in proximity are used, however, close partnerships can be easier to form. Not only is your company a customer to them, your customers are ultimately their customers as well. It has been our experience that working with the supply chain to communicate needs and realities of the marketplace will help alleviate many short-term issues.

Forecasting Frequency

In situations where forecasting is not already part of the culture, it may make sense to begin with a forecast done monthly, extending only three months into the future. In the beginning, this can be performed on a rolling basis going forward and updated perhaps monthly. As time passes, it will probably make sense to update the forecast more frequently. In our experience, what normally happens is that the sales department begins by preparing the forecast once a month and then moves fairly quickly to a more frequent update, such as twice per month and finally once a week. For long lead time items, updating the forecast more often won't make much difference, although perhaps in the case of some unusual short term items that may be coming through and to calculate production capacity, it may provide some advantages.

Managing Big Orders

What happens when an order comes in that's unusually large? Suppose, for example, the usual number in an order is 50 or 100 and an order is received for 1000? This may reserve capacity slots for quite some time. One way to manage this is to split the big order into four or five smaller ones and put each order in production at reasonable distances from one another so that bottlenecks do not occur. The goal is to meet the due date with the last of the divided orders. If this is possible, the delivery of a big order can be done without the disruption such a huge order otherwise would cause. Of course, it will be necessary to coordinate with shipping to make sure the entire order goes out at the same time and is not shipped piecemeal. It may also be necessary to give a heads up to the supply base to insure required materials and components will be available.

Material Usage

How should specialized or long lead time material be assigned to products? Traditionally, if material is in house it's used on a first-come, first-served basis. But this may not be the best methodology for every company, particularly in a highly variable environment that produces a relatively small number of products on a build-to-order basis. If the material was purchased for an order that's anticipated, for example, it probably should not be used for an order that hasn't been forecasted that comes in ahead of it. After all, the material is "assigned" to the anticipated order. This is almost certainly the case if using the materials will cause delivery of that item to be late. If material is ordered for a forecasted job, the material should be designated and clearly indicated as such.

What is the best way to prevent the cannibalization of materials? The only way to insure this does not happen is to have very strict rules and to make everyone aware of the potential negative effects of such actions. Everyone needs to develop and maintain an attitude of service and support toward customers. Without customers there can be no paychecks. Until this is understood, it will be difficult to prevent counterproductive behavior simply by policing it.

Of course exceptions exist to every rule. If your best customer needs something in a hurry and getting it to him or her will mean a delay in delivery for a low-level customer, you may decide to keep your best customer happy. But this should be a conscious and informed decision.

Let's say an order comes in and the sales organization has designated a delivery date based on what the customer wants. Scheduling enters the order and runs software that takes into account material availability required by all orders in hand as well as optimal scheduling through the production process. The result shows that based on prior commitments, the delivery date will not be met.

The software will allow the scheduling function to run "what if" simulations. Perhaps it shows the date can be met if the due date on an already-committed order is moved. In this case, sales should be consulted and a decision made based on what is best for the overall welfare of the company. For example, if the order to be delayed is one replenishing an internal distribution center, the decision to delay it should be obvious.

Scheduling Software

The purchase and installation of the right ERP (Enterprise Resource Planning) scheduling software is critical to the success of build-to-order operations in a highly variable environment. Obviously, this software needs to be able to handle complex product cycles that are variable. Data from a number of areas will determine which program will be best to meet a particular company's needs. The software ought to be able to incorporate bills of materials information, cycle-time data for different products, configurations and subassemblies, and the various routing options through production.

The products we normally deal with are assemblies made up of subassemblies, which in turn are made up of other subassemblies and so on. When we look at product cycles and routings, we think of them as "parents" that have "children," "grand children" and sometimes "great grandchildren." Each represents a different level in the bills of materials. Normally the build for the parents is a sequential activity that takes place as the final assembly.

The children of these assemblies, or grand children, have to be available when needed, and never later or they would bring the flow of production to a halt. In addition, they should not be available too far ahead, or in quantities in excess of what's required. This is a key tenet of Lean production. In certain cases it is literally impossible to have a number of subassemblies built in advance because they may be large. Storage may not be available and to build additional space to house inventory or work-in-process would be costly. This is the case not only for big equipment being manufactured such as airplanes, cars and excavators, but it may also be true for producers of washing machines, air conditioning equipment, chillers, refrigeration machines, and so on.

The final assembly line needs to be loaded so that all stations are always full. The subassembly lines should also be loaded. These must be scheduled by calculating backward from the time each subassembly will be needed in final assembly. The same is true of the subassemblies of subassemblies. This creates a cascading linkage backward in time.

Let us attempt to bring this into focus with an example. Let's say a final assembly line takes subassemblies from three lines. Each has different speeds or takt times, meaning some will have to be started earlier than others. How much in advance will depend on the size of the order. Let's say the final goal is to produce 100 pieces, and it takes one minute to assemble one piece.

Now let's say one of the subassembly lines produces one every two minutes. This line will have to begin 100 minutes before the final assembly line starts. If the order had been for 60 units, it would have to start 60 minutes ahead. The scheduling software must be able to handle this type of variable and this is not common in many software packages.

What happens when a change is made in final assembly? Everything going backward into the subassemblies will have to be changed as well. The software used needs to be capable of making this calculation. On the other hand, it may be possible to move around subassemblies without affecting final assembly as long as they are completed before the time they are needed.

The software also needs to have the ability to check for

all bottlenecks, for materials, and for the availability of capacity. It will be helpful if the software presents output graphically and also if it has a "drag and drop" capability that allows orders to be moved and the effect to be calculated and displayed.

The system also needs to be able to provide alternative recommendations and there should be a "run" mode and a "simulation" mode. This is important since scheduling will often consult with customer service or sales and run a number of "what if" scenarios before a final production strategy is decided upon.

The software should have the capability of dealing creatively with bottlenecks. This is done by defining slack time (queue time) in the cycle associated with a particular product and taking advantage of this. Let's say, for example, that somewhere along the line a particular operation takes ten minutes but a twenty-minute window is available to complete it. This software should be able to use this window to ease a bottleneck situation that would otherwise occur elsewhere.

In cases where different lines are linked directly one to the other, for example, when a subassembly line directly feeds the assembly line and this line feeds the packing area, the software should have the capability of managing buffers between these lines. The size of this buffer will depend on safety stock level requirements and on the differences in takt times between the various subassemblies and final assembly variations.

The software should be capable of running many different types of simulations and "what if" scenarios, and it should be capable of considering multiple constraints at the same time. If there are overloads, for example, and these are created by machines and people, it should be possible to move the machines around to try various configurations, or routings, and then to move people around based on these. The same is true with people and people skills. It should be possible to start by moving people around or by adding them. Then it should also be possible to search for a solution by switching around machines. The best solution that comes from each of these approaches usually will not be the same.

Bills of Materials

Bills of materials (BOMs) need to be accurate, but this is not always easy and many companies have difficulties in this area. Nevertheless, an effort needs to be made to make them accurate and this means someone needs to be held accountable for their accuracy. Not only can inaccuracy cause errors in costing, it can mean required materials will not be ordered with the result that production may not have what it needs to build a product when the time comes to do so.

The first step in making sure bills of materials are accurate is to map the process. How does the company establish a bill of materials? How are part numbers created? Who is responsible? In many companies these functions are not clearly established and defined. Nevertheless, they need to be. Whenever a number of different people are allowed to create part numbers, errors and duplications are almost certain to occur and money is very likely to be wasted.

One of our clients used to allow every engineer to create new part numbers. Often an engineer would decide it was easier to create a new number than to look up an old one even though the product/component may already have had a number. The result was a proliferation of part numbers, many for identical parts. This made ordering parts and the accuracy of BOMs difficult, causing a good deal of waste. To alleviate this, a new process was created. Now a new part number cannot be released until it has passed through a person designated to manage part numbers and corresponding items.

Assuming a great deal of work will be required before bills of materials will be totally accurate, it will be better to have at least somewhat accurate BOMs than to forego the use of scheduling tools. A process should be put in place to progressively make a company's overall BOM universe more accurate. One way to do this is to clean up BOMs by tracking and noting the actual requirements as each parent product is being produced. Care should be taken to insure that any changes made in production as well as in pre and post engineering are thoroughly incorporated into the existing BOMs data base in a timely manner and are also reflected in the "as built" BOMs.

The issue of the number of levels BOMs should have also should be considered. Many times we are asked this question by a customer and, often, there are different points of view. Some people take the position that BOMs should only have one level. Others will include an enormous number of levels.

The number of BOM levels should be a function of scheduling needs. Whenever a need exists to schedule an area of production at finite capacity, a BOM level will have to be created in order to manage it. But if there will not be subassembly inventory and the work center can be assumed as having infinite capacity, it may be possible to avoid creating production orders. In this case, it is enough to create a phase in the routing and, when completed, declare it as closed. This still makes it possible to know where a product is, but it will not allow managing the workload level of each specific work center.

The more the process can be linked together in one continuous flow, the fewer the number of levels that will be needed. In this case, the levels that no longer need to be managed can be turned into "phantoms." Phantoms are part numbers that have no connection to materials resource planning (MRP) so they cannot be in inventory, do not need to be tracked as far as production progress goes, but that have a BOM underneath that MRP explodes to define the purchasing needs. Of course, a Kanban system can also reduce the number of levels required in a BOM, because the material replenishment is done automatically, without the need of the MRP run. From a scheduling point of view, parts pulled by Kanbans are always assumed to be where needed and available for use.

In highly variable environments, however, and in the case of products with long processes that require bulky just-in-time subassemblies, some BOMs levels are required in order to manage production and capacity needs before the main flow begins.

Cycle Times and Routings

Cycle times and routings information is needed for the scheduling software. There has to be enough of this information to manage operations, but sometimes more can be gathered and entered than is necessary. For example, let's say there are four machines in line and the decision is made to consider these four machines as one process because they are always used in combination. This keeps things simple and will work just fine. It will avoid the need for a routing sequence and time to be assigned to each machine. But suppose that later the decision is made to consider one of the machines separately because it now makes sense to replace it with one that is more efficient or faster. When this happens, information can be gathered from the machine and an analysis conducted. Until that time, however, this simply isn't necessary. It boils down to this: a compromise is needed between the "need to have" and the "nice to have" which renders complexity. The need to have is the minimum necessary.

Routings loaded into the software must be accurate and the ERP system has to be able to handle them. But just how accurate do timings have to be? A high degree of accuracy is important if the objective is balancing a line in which movement from one station to the next takes place in short increments of time, such as a few minutes or less. In most highly complex, variable environments, however, assembly operations normally take longer. Cycles for some of our clients range up to seven or eight hours, even though we still measure them in minutes. In such cases, there's usually variability within the process itself.

In repetitive environments, lines need to be balanced. But, as mentioned, in a highly variable environment this may not always be possible. Sometimes production can be more of an art than a carefully planned process. This is especially true when the process depends upon the experience of production operators. Products may be manufactured only once or perhaps only a few times a year. Different products may have different needs with respect to the skills people must have to build them and the amount of time these skills are needed. The bottom line is that the cycle may not be particularly precise. It really doesn't need to be if it takes hours to complete. It may take 400 minutes, for example, or it may take 420 minutes, so the time entered in the schedule might be 410 minutes. That's about seven hours no matter how you look at it. Cycles such as this should be close but do not have to be exact.

It is important to note that, as is the case in traditional Lean environments, there is a need to periodically update cycle times. This activity should be scheduled along with routine, continuous maintenance.

Timely Information of Process Status

The information required by scheduling software needs to be kept up-to-date, which will require data being entered more than once per day. Orders need to be opened and orders need to be closed in a timely manner. It's important to know when raw materials will be in house and available, so the software can calculate when a particular product can be produced. The number of people at work and available time will give the man-hours available. Everything in process and where it stands also has to be kept updated.

When dealing with long activities that take place in each step of process, activities that may last 7 to 8 hours or more, the particular process situation needs to be gathered at the end of the day. Otherwise the scheduling software will calculate that each activity has to start over on the following day, and the production plan won't be accurate.

The scheduler should know what the situation is on the floor at any given moment and should, therefore, spend as much time on the floor as possible in order to stay up to date. Gathering production data can be fairly easy or it can be very complicated, but it makes sense to keep it as simple as possible. Barcoding and a software interface will work perfectly well in most cases. This is a lot less complicated than many people think and will avoid data collection errors.

Time and Data Collection Methods

Production data can also be obtained by filling out time

cards, which is our least preferred method. It can be done by clocking in and out of a job using a PDA or a cell phone if the job location is remote, such as in the case of the construction of a building or an oil rig. An actual time clock in a factory linked to the computer system may be a good solution in some cases. Telephones hooked into the computer system can be used. Or data can be collected by swiping a barcode. Many methods now exist for keeping track of worker and task-related time and activities that will enter the data directly into the ERP and time and attendance systems. Not only can this be linked to payroll, saving a good deal of time and effort in that area, it will provide management and scheduling with real-time, actionable data. Since it's being entered into a computer system, as soon as the data is entered, it's available. On the other hand, it may take weeks for data to be available from old fashion time cards, and these also have to be checked for errors and corrected, which takes up team leaders' time.

The Need to Have a Scheduler on Site

What if a company runs multiple shifts and there is not a scheduler present at each one? This was touched upon earlier. In some companies we do business with it's not unusual for a call to be placed to the scheduler at three in the morning. A better solution of course is to have a scheduler for each shift. But if this isn't practical or possible, it may be that one of the night shift supervisors can be assigned as a back up scheduler. This person will have to go through the training necessary to run the software and to handle the job. He or she will need to be briefed by the dayshift scheduler at the end of that shift. It will also be important to have a set of "what if" rules in place.

What happens when there are other production problems such as engineering errors? Let's say engineering made an error. Maybe the material needed is missing or a subassembly did not arrive. The part-time scheduler should have the authority to take rules-based remedial action when it becomes necessary.

Ramifications of Unforeseen Production Problems

If a hiccup does occur, it may mean skipping to an assembly farther back in the line. For example, suppose a product under construction has arrived at Station B and something is missing. The first reaction may be to move the assembly to Station C to keep the line moving. But certain tasks may need to have been accomplished before the work to be done in Station C. The normal reaction in such situations is to "do whatever we can." In some cases it may not be possible to take a partially produced product out of a line once it has been started. But to continue building just to keep people busy is probably not the best solution. When the goal is to keep people occupied, often inventory is created in the form of partially completed products that will need to be stored somewhere.

The situation described above occurs when Scheduling's rule is to work based on suppliers' promised dates. This means that subassemblies are released for production even though materials for finished goods will arrive later at the promised date. This is normal in long lead time processes. If the complete process takes only a few minutes for each step, we recommend scheduling based only on availability of material. This means that a subassembly will not be released for production until all materials to produce the final product are available.

A case in point has to do with a client we had who believed the first priority was to keep the workers working. Fabric is used in his manufacturing process. Today's unforeseen production problem might be that he has only one of two fabrics needed to produce a particular product that is supposed to be delivered next week. But let's say he also has an order that will require the in-stock fabric, and this one is due in three months. So, to keep people busy, he has them make the one with three months' lead time. Let's say a few days later, the missing fabric arrives. Now he cannot make the order that's due next week because he used it for the one that's not due until three months from now.

When we started working with this client, 20,000 square feet of warehouse space was occupied by products that were partially made. All had been assembled up to a point in order to keep people busy. A major problem with this is that a company doesn't get paid until a product is delivered. This inventory was virtually worthless until it could be transformed into products that could be sold.

Our advice is not to keep people busy just for the sake of it. It's best for the scheduling group to be consulted about the production problem or missing component and for them to reshuffle products in the queue so that manpower and resources can be allocated in the way that will be most productive. The goal should be for the least amount of time and money to be lost. Nevertheless, when production problems occur, it's almost always the case that some people will have to stop and wait until the rest of the line catches up.

By the way, we were able to clear out the 20,000 square feet of inventory. First, we made a list of all the items and what was needed to complete each one. Then we coordinated with the supplier to deliver the pieces that were missing. Then the factory finished each one. During this time, we worked with the supplier, explained the situation and stressed the importance of delivering just what was needed — no more and no less. Once the supplier's awareness was raised, the problem went away. Inventory has now been drawn down to zero and because of better coordination with the supplier, this plant has not made any partially completed goods. Clear communication was fundamental in solving this production problem.

The supplier simply had not understood the company's operation and its requirements. Now, rather than having inventory piled up, the plant starts each day with a one hour buffer to allow for machine failures and other issues. Often, at the end of the day, this one-hour buffer of inventory has been used up.

Recap

Complex and variable, build-to-order environments will typically have many different machines and potential processes available, not all of which may be used every day. Indeed, each day may be quite different from the next in terms of the configurations of product moving through the production process.

A goal of any Lean Manufacturing operation is to eliminate as much wasted effort and downtime as possible and to keep product moving through value-added steps at a pace equal to the drumbeat of the marketplace. To keep product flowing requires a sophisticated and centralized scheduling process that uses scheduling software to determine the best sequence for products to be assembled on a given day so that as little downtime as possible occurs. The timing of the construction of subassemblies as well as the arrival of components and materials all must be coordinated. Workers need to be positioned at the correct work center where they will perform specific tasks at specific points in time. This requires a centralized scheduling function and a scheduler who generates efficient work assignments using computer software. This person must keep everyone informed and up to date concerning the schedule, which may change throughout the day as production problems occur.

This means what supervisors have historically done must change. Rather than scheduling the work themselves, they now must become expediters and facilitators whose job is to meet the production requirements in an efficient manner.

Calculating delivery dates can be tricky in such an environment and this must be performed by scheduling. Orders may need to be prioritized, of course, and this should be done in consultation with customer service or sales.

In seasonal environments where some products are built to forecast up to the point of customization, such platforms are managed like an accordion, i.e., accumulated when demand is lowest and depleted during the peak season. Large orders can cause scheduling issues and are often best handled by breaking them into smaller, more manageable orders spaced at reasonable intervals. This needs to be coordinated with shipping and customer service. Long lead time components need to be managed carefully and controls should be put in place so that those earmarked for use to build specific products are not cannibalized.

The purchase and installation of the right scheduling software is critical to the success of a business operating in a highly variable environment. This software has to be able to handle complex product cycles that are variable. It will need to be able to incorporate bills of materials information, cycle-time data for different products, configurations and subassemblies, and the various routing options through production. In addition, many complex products are made up of subassemblies, which in turn are made up of other subassemblies and so on. All need to arrive in final assembly at the right times. Scheduling software needs to be able to accommodate this.

What happens when a change is made in final assembly? Everything going backward into the subassemblies must change and the software needs to be capable of making this calculation. The software needs to:

• check for bottlenecks, for materials, and for availability of capacity.

• present output graphically and have a "drag and drop" capability, allowing orders to be moved and the effect displayed.

• be able to deal creatively with bottlenecks by defining slack times and/or queue times in various product cycles and taking advantage of these.

• have a run mode and a simulation mode so that "what if" scenarios can be viewed.

• be capable of calculating outcomes based on moving machines, changing routings and by adding or moving people.

Bills of material (BOMs) must be accurate and this can be done by mapping the process of creating them. The number of levels of BOMs depends on scheduling needs. Kanban systems can reduce this because parts on Kanban are assumed always to be available from a scheduling point of view.

Cycle times and routings are needed for scheduling software. Time and activity data can be gathered in many ways including PDAs and cell phones for remote jobs and time clocks and barcodes in factories. Many methods now exist.

There has to be enough of this information to manage but care needs to be taken not to make it more complex than necessary since it needs to be kept up to date. For example, if four machines in line perform one process in combination, only one routing is needed to account for this.

Long activities that may run over into the following day need to be factored in at the end of each day in order to be taken into account in the next day's schedule. The scheduler should know what the production situation is at any given moment and spend as much time on the floor as possible.

Chapter Four: Supporting the Build-to-Order Operation

In a repetitive environment, each workstation needs a consistent supply of materials and this is usually not a complicated task. Materials are used and they are replenished. This can often be done through the use of Kanbans, which are cards or signals sent to material supply and sometimes directly to suppliers, indicating what is needed. On the other hand, in a highly variable environment some materials may be used repetitively such as fasteners or brackets but many other materials may not, making material supply a more complicated issue.

Material handlers need to have the right materials ready and in place when the time comes for a changeover. For this reason, they not only need a schedule to follow, it may also be helpful to give them templates which indicate the materials that will be needed in each case. This template or diagram should include details such as the order in which materials are used and the exact location to place them in the production environment. As items in process change, materials that are no longer needed must be removed and the right materials for what's coming next put in place, based on a different location map or template. This is part of the setup process.

Obviously, materials management's job is to insure that what is needed is on hand when it is needed and where it is needed. But our experience has been this often does not happen as it should. Materials may arrive late or may have quality problems, or perhaps sufficient quantities are not available. Sometimes, a required material or item may have arrived and those who need it aren't aware because it wasn't processed properly through in the receiving area.

In addition, material handling personnel need to keep Scheduling informed when things go awry so that the product mix and sequence can be reshuffled as necessary. This means inputting data into software frequently to keep it up to date. It should go without saying that if scheduling software has incorrect data, all its calculations will be wrong.

Kitting Materials

Kitting is normally a non-value added activity. However, in some cases, such as when parts are bulky and can not be stored next to the line or when materials arrive in bulky quantities and need to be split between different lines, a way to supply the right materials in the right configurations is to "kit" them. Kits may be placed in carts or bins that can be moved into place. These carts need to be assembled in a thought out and methodical way so that assembly time isn't lost searching for a part. Suffice it to say, the right parts need to be at hand at the appropriate time.

One may wish to view a kit as a subassembly since lead time is required to build the kit and it has to arrive at a specific place ahead of the time that it is needed. This under-

Fig. 16 — Example of kitting of bulky components

lines the need for a schedule of the timing and sequence of the various products to be produced on a given day to be published and distributed well ahead.

Specific individuals should be devoted to this process in

order for them to become proficient at it. Operators must not to be required to pull together or search for materials because this takes them away from value-added work.

Dealing with Big Material Items

One of our clients produces a product that moves through two prep stations and four workstations. Each product is quite large and is made up of forty or fifty components. Some of these components are big and heavy. They must be moved on pallets. Because of their size, not enough room is available on the line to place pallets of components for more than one variation of the product at a time. The result is, when the product changes, parts pallets must be changed. A forklift is required to accomplish this, which means that changing an entire line can be difficult and time consuming. In addition, a particular order may require several variations of the product, making material handling a significant issue.

The way we have solved this is by kitting the various parts based on what is called for to fill each order. So if six units of one kind are being built, the kit will contain six motors, six coils, six frames and so forth. Multiple orders can also be handled up to a point. Perhaps six of one unit will be made, three of another and four of another. Kits will be put together with six of each item required for the first, three of each for the second, and four of each for the fourth. All of the parts will be labeled and arranged in the order in which the parts will be used.

Providing the Right Tools

Tools are another consideration in that many more may be required in a complex-variable environment than in a repetitive one. It's important to place or arrange them in a location after careful evaluation of how and when they will be used. Tools should not be hidden away in a box. A careful analysis of where and how to store them can avoid waste because time will not be lost in locating them. One approach we suggest is to use tool trees or tool boards. This can even

Fig. 17 — Tools shadow board

be handled in work environments where tools tend to disappear. For example, there may be a form signed by the facilitator or the supervisor of a line at the beginning of each shift that he or she has received all the expected tools. In this case, shift personnel should not be released until all tools have been accounted for.

Various tasks may sometimes require different tools than may normally be stored in a particular workstation. These, too, need to be arranged and organized to be accessible in a way that will result in maximum efficiency. In cases where

Fig. 17A — Tools shadow board

tools are brought to a workstation, the responsibility of the material handler or facilitator is to place them in the defined and proper locations.

One English facility we know of has a separate tool board for the tools required for each build process performed in the plant. In this way, a new kit doesn't have to be created each time it's needed. These boards are positioned at the appropriate workstation by rolling them into place just before they will be needed. This saves a great deal of time because the right tools for a job are all together and don't have to be rounded up.

Whether or not this is practical will depend on how many duplicate sets of tools will be required and how much they cost. The cost of kitting needs to be weighed against the cost of tool duplication. Kitting will, of course, take place each and every time a particular set is needed.

In devising a plan for making tools easily accessible and in good working order, it's important to consider if there are special needs for power tools. For example, if they are battery powered or have a charger, it will be important to have extra batteries on hand or to have a way to make sure the tool is charged regularly. A line can be brought to a halt by tool with a dead battery or one in which the charge has run out. It can be quite frustrating when dozens of people have to wait because a relatively inexpensive battery is not readily available.

Purchasing

The function of purchasing is to negotiate with suppliers the conditions of the supply. This includes prices, delivery, methods of transportation, packaging, methods of communication between the two companies, quality, reliability and performance. But this is the extent of it. Everything else to do with material supply should be in the hands of scheduling or material supply and these functions need to be local. In a case where multiple plants exist, the purchasing function may be centralized but material supply and scheduling need to be on site at each plant in order to control the inventory required to keep the plant producing and meeting its due dates. Even when most purchasing is centralized and master contracts are issued for plant consumables such as office supplies, toilet paper and so forth, it probably makes sense for the actual purchase of these items to be made locally. The same is true with shipper and freight forwarders. Master contracts on rates may be centralized but the decision concerning which to use for a particular order is usually best left at the local level. Purchasing should also maintain constant contact with Scheduling and materials planning. Even though it is Materials Planning or Sourcing that manages the day-to-day needs for the production process, some of the issues that arise in the relationship with suppliers require communication with Purchasing, and in some of these cases, Purchasing will need to communicate with Materials Planning. Although these are two different organizations, communications between them and all the parties involved must be fluid.

Purchasing in a complex environment is more difficult than in a traditional environment due to the small lot sizes and the need to produce parts on design specs. Suppliers will many times be small and flexible. They will most likely be located next to or in close proximity to the plant, and a relation of close partnership with them should be the norm.

Another critical activity Purchasing should periodically undertake is the updating of lead times and costs.

Engineering

It makes sense to take a hard look at the engineering process and how it might be improved, particularly when a good deal of custom engineering is required for built-to-order products.

The engineered-to-order (ETO) and build-to-order production situations are similar. Production has a number of products it needs to produce. Engineering has a stack of orders it needs to address. The product that engineering turns out consists of a drawing and a bill of materials. The same sort of variations exist in accomplishing this as in the custom order production environment. The time it takes to complete a task on one type of job can be extremely different — longer or shorter — than on a different type of job.

Just as production will benefit from instituting the primary step of order, cleanliness and safety, engineering will benefit from standardizing information and organizing in such a way that everyone will be able to quickly find what's needed. Engineers should not have to start from scratch or cover old ground each time.

From a cultural standpoint, it's human nature for engineers and others in what might be termed "creative" positions to want to reinvent the wheel each time a new project comes through the door. But in reality it is much more efficient and can even lead to significantly higher product quality and durability to reuse knowledge which has been gained and used successfully in similar situations. This is certainly one key to Toyota's success in product development.

But for such a situation to work, the right tools are required, which in this case means a system must be devised to gather and store knowledge in a way that makes that knowledge readily obtainable and usable. This will allow a company to standardize parts, components and subassemblies, which is almost certain to lead to greater efficiency. Otherwise an engineer will likely design a part or spend time developing a control or switch or subassembly that may already exist. Valuable time will have been lost reinventing a wheel and even more time may be lost later because retooling may be required to accommodate the new part or subassembly.

Just as a way needs to be found to capture what has worked in a given situation so it can easily be reused, what doesn't work or has become obsolete needs to be systematically weeded out of this data base to make the data practical and easy to use. We mention this because we've often found that companies are generally very good at creating data and often not very good cleaning up and eliminating data that's no longer used or necessary.

Visuals can be used in Engineering to communicate scheduling and where things stand, including the number of jobs in the works and due dates. In the area of flow, some companies have found it makes sense to organize Engineering so that different engineers review different aspects of custom jobs moving through. One might review the electrical aspects, another the mechanical and so forth. This can speed up the process and take advantage of the skills and knowledge of those most qualified in each area.

A ETO Case History

Here's how ETO worked in one client company. Jobs would come in and be assigned to different engineers by the department manager. An engineer would look at what the customer wanted and then search for a similar drawing and bill of materials in his computer. He would print these out and make changes on them by hand. Scribbled-on pieces of paper would then be sent to a secretary who was shared by everyone in the department. It was her job to convert these scribbles into revised documents. This not only created a bottleneck, errors would inevitably come about as a result.

Another way errors frequently happened was that the engineers had two separate systems — one for drawings and the other for bills of materials. These did not communicate with one another. An engineer would pull up a drawing, print it out, then close out that software program and open another to find a bill of materials that could serve as a template for the job. As might be suspected, what was called for by the drawing did not always match the bill of materials. Clearly the two needed to be part of the same system so that software would check and double check the accuracy of both.

When drawings and bills of materials make it into production containing errors, all kinds of problems are likely to occur. Materials may not be available when needed. Something may get assembled and then have to be disassembled because a subassembly is missing. Once a product gets out into the market and then comes back for service the materials and parts used based on the drawings and bill of materials may not match what is actually there. The list goes on.

The first step in correcting this was to purchase new software that integrated drawings and bills of materials. This software included as much built-in poka yoke (mistake proofing) as possible. For example, it is now impossible to create a product that does not have certain components. Obvious examples are that a lamp needs to have a light bulb and a car must have at least four tires and a spare.

Next was to divide the process into two phases. The first was for new drawings and bills of materials to be created using software templates for families of product configurations. The second was for the output from this phase to be checked for accuracy and completeness by a different engineer than the one who created it. Anyone who has tried to proofread a report, essay or book they have written knows that it is often difficult to spot mistakes or errors in his or her own work.

There also needs to be a scheduling function in ETO operations. The fact is many of the same concepts apply that have been covered for scheduling of assembly and production. Due dates will be required for custom-engineered products so that they can be manufactured in time to meet committed dates.

Let's say two jobs have the same due date, but one will require 12 hours of engineering time and the other 24. Obviously the one requiring 24 hours will have to be placed ahead in line. Unless there is a clear determination of which project is next, however, when an engineer finishes a project he or she may pick the project he likes best rather than the next in line. Or he might take one that's easier to complete, or a small one he/she can finish before going home if it is near the end of the day.

New Product Development

It's important to have a methodical process in place for engineering to customize existing products. But a rigidly-controlled process can sometimes be counterproductive when it comes to developing brand new products. Toyota, for example, takes a nonlinear approach to product development and this has proved to be much more productive than the linear systems used by most American companies. A study conducted by the National Center for Manufacturing Science (NCMS) indicates that Toyota's development engineers are four times more productive on average than their American and European counterparts. That is, they spend four times more time adding value — a total of 80 percent as opposed to 20 percent.

As with the Toyota production system, the basic goal in new product development at Toyota is to eliminate waste or "muda." With 80 percent of engineers' time spent adding value, the NCMS study reveals that Toyota has done a superb job in this regard. According to Michael N. Kennedy, who wrote a book about the Toyota development system called *Product Development for the Lean Enterprise,* the reason is that Western systems follow an approach that focuses engineers on individual tasks and due dates for each new model under development, which among other things involves a good deal of bureaucratic red tape. Toyota does not focus its efforts on the development of specific vehicles or on individual tasks but rather on the development of the many subsystems that come together to form automobiles and trucks. The result is Toyota engineers are less concerned with details such as completing drawings, schematics and all the many bureaucratic tasks normally associated with product development. They concentrate instead on developing superior subsystems and components in the belief these subsystems can be mixed and matched to create a whole host of new product possibilities. They also have a system in place to capture knowledge, to reuse what worked in the past and to avoid stumbling down a path previously explored that had proved to be unproductive. Kennedy calls the Toyota system a "knowledge-based system," as opposed to the western system, which he labels a "process-based system." The knowledge created by Toyota's engineers is captured in a data base that's made available to everyone in Toyota product development with the goal of eliminating duplication of efforts. The reinventing of wheels each time a new vehicle is developed is viewed as muda. Reusing knowledge is one way muda is eliminated.

Sales

As previously stated, Sales has an important role in providing the factory with the required information to allow for preparatory activities to be performed. Based on forecast data:

• the factory can be staffed with the right number of workers and the right equipment acquired, ahead of time,

• agreements with potential subcontractors can be negotiated to meet pick demand needs

• Purchasing can organize agreements with suppliers in order to be sure that long lead time items will be delivered on time.

But the forecast it provides isn't the only way Sales affects the rest of the plant. Sales can impact costs and factory behaviors in other ways. In electronics, for example, there is often the issue of the minimum number of pieces to be produced. In this environment, as in many others, a set up cost must be amortized over each piece. Moreover, products often have small dimensions not easy to be manipulated in the equipment. So, engineers design boards with a number of products on them (2, 3, 6, 9, 20, and so forth). A company needs to clearly define how to handle this. Sales needs to communicate to customers the minimum acceptable order quantity, or what the extra cost will be if the quantity ordered is less than the minimum. So that there are no surprises, Sales should be involved when decisions such as this are made, and it should support them in the outside world.

Quality and Continuous Process Improvement

Quality inspection on raw materials in a highly variable environment is not an easy task. In these environments, assessing the quality of raw materials and components or subassemblies received from sub-suppliers can be difficult. New materials are often introduced, especially in ETO environments, and Quality needs to know what the critical dimensions are that must be checked. Instructions cannot be prepared for each new part, of course, but standardized check forms should be created in order to allow incoming materials inspectors to verify that the material is in accordance with specifications. These forms are also needed in production because they are a tool each operator can use to assess his or her own job.

In a variable environment people often do not perform the same tasks repeatedly. They do different things at different times, and this can lead to quality verification issues. Let's say workstation three puts the tires on and station four verifies this has been done. This check or verification becomes routine. But now let's say that because the environment is variable, station three does not always put the tires on. Instead, station six sometimes performs this task. It will then become station seven's job to verify the tires are on. But if this happens only once in a while, the operator at station seven may not remember to do this job.

For this reason it's important to limit the number of variations in tasks to the full extent possible. The operators must have a quality check sheet that is particular to each item coming through. This document needs to be attached to and flow with the item being manufactured. As a double check the next station needs to verify that all the tasks on the check sheet have been performed.

There should also be a testing process as the final step for those products for which this makes sense. The issues that testing turns up should be accumulated for each classification, type, or variation of item produced. These should be assembled into a data base for a Pareto analysis that reveals the recurring issues for each product variation that must be resolved.

Not all the issues that become part of this data base will have to do with quality. Some may have to do with repeated delay issues and missing components. Whatever the case may be, having this information and dealing with recurring issues should be part of the continuous improvement component of the Lean initiative.

How can such information be used to eliminate quality issues? By using an analysis Toyota people refer to "The Five Why's," it is possible to get to the root cause of a problem. One needs to ask "Why?" at least five times in sequence. This is like peeling away the layers of an onion. For example, a capillary tube soldered to a bellows leaks:

- Why does it leak?
The welding does not seal properly.
- Why does the welding not seal properly?
There is a deposit of a material inside the capillary tube.
- Why is there a deposit inside the capillary tube?
Washing of the tube did not clean it.
- Why did washing not clean it?
The detergent used was not working effectively.
- Why did the detergent not work effectively?
*The detergent formula was not effective on this
particular type of deposit.*

Many companies will collect Pareto analysis data and do very little with it. But recurring problems cost time and money. Continuous process improvement requires the systematic removal of impediments to quality and to the maintenance of takt time. In our experience, such analyses should be performed daily if necessary in order to eliminate these impediments.

Input from Workers Must Be Used

If operators write down problems which have occurred in the space provided on white boards giving daily or hourly objectives and nothing is done about these problems, the operators will soon stop going to the trouble to do so. For example, sometimes a cell will not meet its takt time and will not do so consistently, yet no one will say anything about this. It is the responsibility of the line leaders to take the

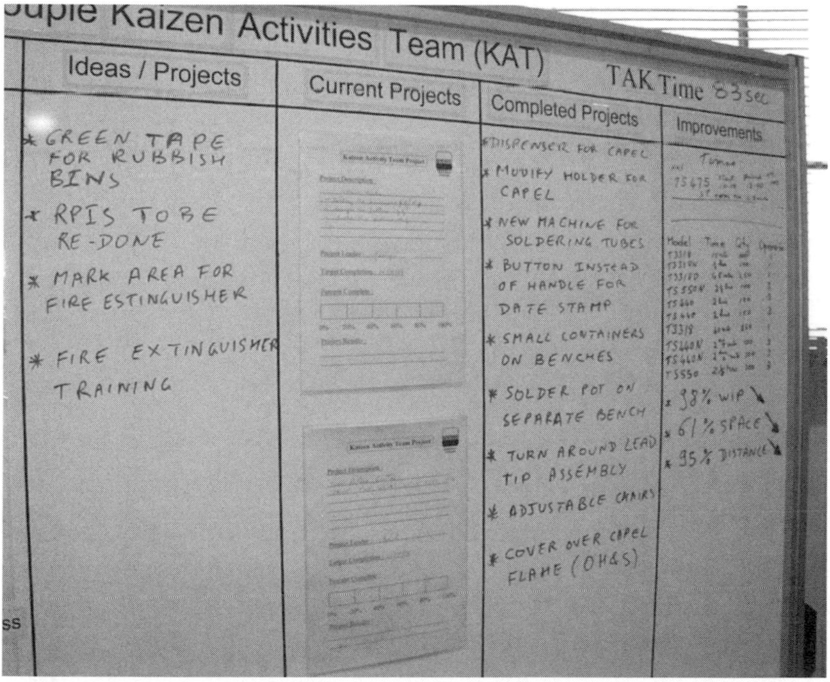

Fig. 18— Workers' suggestions and follow up actions

information and to deal with it, which usually means a root-cause analysis needs to be performed in order to determine the cause of the concern or problem.

In many cases, production cells and representatives of the various support departments such as Purchasing, Material Handling and Process Engineering meet at the start of a shift and again at the end. This is a good time to deal with issues that have caused delays or with other disruptions that have arisen. Assignments need to be made concerning who will deal with each issue. One to do with materials may be assigned to Purchasing. One to do with engineering should be dealt with by Engineering and so forth. These representatives should be required, usually within 48 hours, to report what has been done to alleviate the issue.

Poka Yoke

Poka Yoke, or mistake proofing, is also an important quality tool. Mistake proofing means that the product and the process are designed so that a mistake cannot occur. The connectors on a personal computer illustrate a type of mistake proofing. Try to insert the printer cable or the display cable the wrong way, and you will find you can't. The connector is shaped so that only one orientation is possible.

Here's another example. A plastic part was held in place by four pegs, two at top and two at bottom. All four pegs were the same size, so it was possible to install the part upside down. By making one of the bottom pegs larger than the others, correct assembly was assured every time.

During the design phase, engineers must insure that parts cannot be assembled incorrectly. This is the easiest and least costly approach to quality. Nonetheless, mistake proofing must be carried into the manufacturing process, particularly when it has not been part of the design process for products already in production. This may not be easy since many products in the variable environment may be produced only occasionally or perhaps only once. One way is through simple visuals that allow employees to see how a job should be done. This can be very important because of employee turnover. Some of our clients have rates as high as 55 percent turnover per annum. This is a common problem in low cost countries where industry is only beginning to take hold and people often are on the look out for other ways to make a living. With a rate this high, a company is in a permanent training mode.

Of course, most companies would like to solve the problem of turnover. But in many cases this issue exists because of a company's autocratic culture and lack of worker empowerment, and this is not something that can be solved overnight. Most certainly, strong leadership training programs need to be put in place. Team leaders will have to be taught to become coaches rather than dictators so that team members feel empowered and that they are making important contributions to the organization. As time goes by, attitudes will change and workers will develop a sense of loyalty and esprit de corps. Then they won't be so quick to leave. Even so, because new workers will have to be trained constantly and frequently until a new culture takes hold, processes should be broken down into simple activities that can be learned quickly. In addition, documentation, diagrams, templates and instructions must be simple and easy to understand.

The Importance of Standardization

Just as there are many ways to skin a cat, there usually are many ways to do a task. It's human nature for different people to have different ways of doing things. Even so, to maintain high quality, everyone who performs a particular job must perform it in the same way. Even though some people may resist, this needs to be enforced to insure the time it takes to do a job and the quality of the output remain constant. If a better way can be demonstrated, then everyone needs to change to the new approach. This ought to be handled at the production team level. Someone on the team should be the "owner" of each process and these process owners need to be the guardians of the process and the ones to explain it to other team members who need to be able to perform it.

In some cases, the time required for tasks to be performed during a sequence at a workstation may mean an operator needs more than one day to complete the work, making it difficult to monitor progress. A way to deal with this is to have the high level standardized work instructions divided into parts by day. Detailed standardized work instructions should be made available for each high level activity. If the work at a

Seq.		D/L Productivity = 80%			End time	End time
		LT cum	Oper. 1	Oper. 2	Day 1	Day 2
		min	min	min		
1	Hose Connections from Compressed Air System to Hammer head connection in Mast	46	46.3	44	07:10-08:00	
2	Hose connection from engine pump to oil-filter and oil pump to oil tank	70	24.1	21		
3	Hose connection from hand pump to filter on top of oil tank	80	9.6	8		
4	Hose connection from cooler to filter on the top of oil tank	87	6.5	7		
5	Place connector on P, place connector on T and connect hose from MDV to oil cooler	101	13.1	14	08:50	
6	Hose connection from 1st Manifold to rodrack (to lifting)	112	10.2	11		
7	Hose connection from 1st Manifold to rodrack (to sliding)	123	10.2	11		
8	Hose connection from 1st Manifold to Front Left Leg	143	19.6	0		
9	Hose connection from 1st Manifold to Front Rigth Leg	143	0.0	20		
10	Hose connection from 1st Manifold to Brake Clamp	150	7.3	8		
11	Hose connection from 1st Manifold to Rotation Clamp (brake)	158	7.3	8		
12	Hose connection from 2nd Manifold to Rotation Clamp (rotation)	165	7.3	8	10:00	
13	Hose connection from 2nd Manifold to Odex	173	7.3	8		
14	Hose connection from 2nd Manifold to Mast movement (sliding)	180	7.3	8		
15	Hose connection from 2nd Manifold to Mast movement (rotation)	192	11.0	12		
16	Hose connection from 2nd Manifold to Mast movement (lifting)	203	11.0	12	10:40	
17	Hose connection from 2nd Manifold to Rear Right Leg and Rear Left Leg	241	37.5	37		
18	Hose connection from MDV to Mast Rotary head sliding	261	20.4	19	12:00	
19	Hose connection from Main Distribution Valve MDV to Rotary head rotation	293	31.5	31		
20	Hose connection from Left Crawler to MDV	313	20.6	21	13:00	
21	Hose connection from Rigth Crawler to MDV	334	20.6	21		
22	Hose connection from 1st Manifold to 2nd Manifold (P and T)	334	20.0	0		
23	Hose connection from MDV to Weld Machine	356	0.0	22		
24	Hose connection from MDV to Sloop Winch (super winch)	399	24.6	42	14:00	
25	Hose connection from MDV to Water Pump (Mix Pump)	399	17.5	0		
26	Hose connection from Mast holder to Oil tank	406	0.0	8		
27	Preparation of cooler collector of low pressure (CC)	406	6.9	0		
28	Hose connection from MDV to Main Hoist in Mast	430	23.8	18	14:50	
29	Hose connection from Hammer Head Lubrication Pump to MDV	21	0.0	17		
30	Hose connection to Hand Pump (rif.57)	25	15.1	0		
31	Hose connection from MDV to P-line of 1st manifold	38	0.0	16		

Fig. 19 — High level standardized work instructions divided by day

139

Installation of Hydraulic Hoses from mast piston/direction to top

	Operator A sec	Operator B sec
"study" the scheme	30.0	
get a big hose 3/4" (number 42)	30.0	
wait for 1st person to finish		60.0
install the hose on steel tube on the side of the mast	30.0	30.0
get 2 installation plates (rif.52) and 4 bolts, 1 O ring, allen wrench	60.0	60.0
apply Oring between hose and valve and fit hose to steering valve on top of mast	240.0	240.0
attach with 2 installations plates, boths hose to valve and tighten		
leave the 2nd edge of hose free		
look at the scheme	20.0	
get 2 hoses 3/8" (number 21,22)	30.0	
wait for 1st person to finish		50.0
install 2 hoses on steel tube on the side of the mast	60.0	60.0
get the wrench	30.0	
remove 2 blind nuts from the mast holder	30.0	
attach 2 hoses into mast holder and tighten	120.0	
get wrench		30.0
remove 2 plastic plugs from the main hoist		10.0
attach other edge of 2 hoses into valve of main hoist/winch and tighten		120.0
look at the scheme	20.0	
get 1 hose (1/4") (number 123)	30.0	
wait for 1st person to finish		50.0
install 1 hose through steel bar to valve on the top of the mast		90.0
attach 1 hose into valve (rif.40) port-E on the top of the mast and tighen	90.0	120.0
get the wrench	30.0	
remove 1 blind nuts from the mast holder	30.0	
attach 1 hose into mast holder and tighten	120.0	
look at the scheme		20.0
get 1 hose (3/8") (number 48)		30.0

Fig. 20 — Detailed standardized work instructions

station requires more than one day and a need exists to handle very large materials, it may be necessary to feed materials to the various workstations according to the sequence order and the day the materials will be required. This will mean a determination must be made of the point reached in each cycle and the associated materials needed during each day of each phase. BOMs should also be structured accordingly. This is particularly important in engineered products (BTO, ETO) where a basic cycle/BOM structure can be defined.

Recap

Material handlers need to have the right materials ready and in place when the time arrives for a changeover. To do so they must have a schedule and may require templates or diagrams showing the correct items and precise locations. Kitting may also make sense, particularly when materials are large, since these can be made up ahead of time and moved into place on carts.

The right tools also need to be available when needed. These can also be placed by material handlers. Tool trees or tool boards may make sense in environments where tools tend to disappear. Each new shift can sign for them. Boards containing the specific tools to perform a particular build process might also be put on wheels so they can be rolled into place when and where needed.

Purchasing needs to negotiate the conditions of supply but Material Supply (Sourcing or Expediting) and Scheduling located at the plant site should control the inventory needed to keep the plant producing and meeting due dates.

Engineering to order (ETO) is very similar to build to order (BTO) and similar scheduling techniques should be used to maintain flow and takt time in this area. A system should be devised to gather, store and reuse knowledge in a way that makes it readily available to all who need it. Part numbers need to be standardized to eliminate duplicates and engineering software needs to be integrated with bills of materials. As much poka yoke as possible should be built into engineering software. It should automatically check, for example, that all required parts are present. (A lamp must have a bulb.)

Typically people don't do the same tasks repeatedly in a variable environment. To help operators perform the different tasks associated with different products, there should be a quality check sheet that accompanies each item moving through. As a double-check the operator of a station following an operation or series of operations should check to be sure each was performed properly. A process to capture information on issues that arise should be in place and root cause analyses should be employed in the ongoing continuous improvement effort. It should go without saying that input from workers must be used or they will become discouraged and stop making suggestions. Poka yoke (mistake proofing) should be part of the design process and carried into manufacturing as well. One way is through simple visuals. Standardization of work is also important to insure quality. There should be an owner of each process and he or she should teach the process to others who need to know it.

Chapter Five: Bringing About Change

Management by fear and intimidation can be the biggest impediment to a Lean transformation and can have other repercussions, including a high turnover rate. We've seen turnover rates as high as 70 percent a year because of it.

A company that is ruled by fear not only has difficulty retaining employees but those that stick around are less motivated to work and are certainly not motivated to take the initiative. It's also highly unlikely they will report the true cause of problems that arise. Obviously in such a situation, a strong need for change exists.

When the autocratic management is withdrawn, however, workers will not suddenly change and start taking initiative. What typically happens is that the old saying "when the cat's away the mice will play" goes into effect. The result is that changing the culture and the empowering of workers is almost always a long term proposition. The quickest we've seen it happen was over a period of six months. In this case, an enormous change was brought about primarily because the top executive at the facility — who'd been an autocrat — was replaced by an individual who managed by walking around, seeing the issues, and interacting with the work force. He was also a great listener.

It was that simple.

It All Starts at the Top

This brings us to a point we have attempted to make many times. Change will not take place if the person in charge doesn't really want it or see the value in it. The culture of an organization is established at the top. If the top doesn't want to change — if the top people do not actually change their ways — nothing will happen. And when they do change and begin acting differently, training and coaching will still be required and may need to continue for a year or more.

The company we referred to that was able to change quickly had been run by a man who intimidated everyone. He'd even dress down his subordinates in the presence of others. Everyone was afraid to volunteer information or to make suggestions. But even if they had done so, it wouldn't have mattered. He made all the decisions and demanded his orders be carried out to the letter. The only way for the transformation of the facility he'd been running to move forward was for him to be replaced.

Fortunately the new man put in charge was his exact opposite. He was a listener, very approachable and open. From day one he spent most of his day walking around, talking to people, finding out what was on their minds, listening to their suggestions and implementing those that made sense. People responded to this. They quickly saw that things could be different. The oppressive atmosphere lifted like morning fog on a hot summer day.

Physical Changes Mirror Psychological Ones

The factory mentioned above, which is an eighty thousand square foot facility, had been impossible to walk through. Trash, empty boxes and scrap were everywhere. The floor was covered with oil drippings. This was the first thing to undergo a profound transformation. During the last two weeks of one year and the first two weeks of the following year, the entire production floor was revamped. Lines were reconfigured to allow maximum capability for customization, while maximizing efficiency. More than a third of the space formerly used for manufacturing was freed up and would now be used for a new line of products to be put in place.

We thought it would take a long time to get everything back up to speed. For one thing, the union was resisting the proposed changes and the new production goals. Bad feelings ran high because of the old autocratic management style. This union could have made things very difficult and probably would have if the old manager had still been in charge. But he was not and the new man stepped in and spoke with union leaders. He spoke with workers. Carefully, calmly and with convincing empathy, he explained what was at stake for the company and its workers. He outlined how the changes could and would work to everyone's benefit. He convinced them what was being offered was a win-win-win situation. The company would benefit. The company's customers would benefit. And the company's workers would benefit.

Things Ramp Up in a Hurry

Everything was up to speed one week after the factory floor was converted and people were back at work. We can even say that it was more than up to speed. Output was up by 50 percent even though the number of people was the same.

Some may be tempted to view this as a short term phenomenon, but the truth is that this increase has been sustained. Whereas the factory had been struggling to keep up and often had fallen behind, its capacity now exceeds current needs. Management has actually taken steps to pace the rate of production.

This remarkable turnaround happened because people wanted it to happen. They wanted the transformation to be successful and were committed to it because they liked their new boss and wanted to give him their support. And they also knew it would be in their own interest for the transformation to succeed. We are convinced it would not have taken place if the old boss had remained in his position.

Different Countries, Different Cultures

The transformation described above took place in a developed country. In the more than dozen years we've been in this line of work, we have often been involved with clients who operate in the same industries, making similar products and yet have found their transformations to Lean have been very different. We have, for example, implemented a transformation in the United Kingdom and one in Egypt in which the processes were identical. Yet there were differences in how the two Lean transformations played out. Another transformation involved similar processes in Romania and in Italy.

In Romania, as in Italy, the processes to be implemented were state of the art. But people did not have the background of exposure to advanced technology to easily support this. Consider, for example, the technology level in the United States and in other developed countries. In the U.S. you can check yourself out at many grocery stores. You simply follow the menu — scan the merchandise yourself, bag the items, select the form of payment you prefer and swipe your credit card or enter cash and receive change. In Romania such things simply do not happen. The result was that supervisors and workers were seeing many things for the first time. What was being introduced to them represented a quantum leap. We've found that in these circumstances workers will ultimately "get it" but it will take time. Patience and systematic, continuous training is required.

In less developed countries, particularly in rural areas, additional issues arise. There may be a harvest time or a hunting season. People may leave the plant one day and simply not come back. Or if they do, it may be two months later.

There are environments where it is very difficult to teach people to take initiative because they have always been told what to do. These may have been highly autocratic environments where individual accountability did not exist. For people with such backgrounds to be fully productive in a

148

Lean environment, they must be taught to think and to participate and this takes time and effort because it represents such a big cultural shift. Some will simply do not want to take on responsibility.

How can this be overcome?

It will probably take training by industrial psychologists, which will include role playing and acting out. It also may help to institute the use of action reports in conjunction with team meetings.

Action Reports Make People Accountable

Let's say pre and post production meetings are held each day and quality or engineering or supply issues arise and these are assigned to individuals in each area to take care of. But suppose those assigned do nothing. They aren't used to being accountable, and they don't want to start being accountable now. One possibility is to use action reports.

An action report is similar to the minutes of a meeting, except that it leaves out superfluous discussion and zeros in on decisions made and actions to be taken. It can be very brief. It lists the action items, states specifically the individual who is to take action on each and the deadline agreed upon. An action report can be sent out to all involved in paper form or electronically.

It's one thing to tell a team member he or she is accountable for an action. It's another for him or her to take this seriously. With action reports, accountability is in black and white. Nothing could be clearer because it's right there on paper. No question about accountability can possibly exist. By using them, team leaders no longer must rely only on those they feel they can depend on.

Action reports contribute to team meeting effectiveness. Meetings begin with a review of items that should have been completed. When someone is called on to report and no action has been taken, he or she will be subject to the scrutiny of others. This is usually enough to get people to take action and be prepared.

Meetings conclude with a review of new action items identified during the meeting, verification of who is responsible for each action and agreement on target completion dates and the expected outcome. If someone doesn't think he can get a particular item completed in the allotted time, that person needs to say so along with the reason why. Then a different date can be negotiated and agreed upon. Also, if something unforeseen comes up between meetings and an item is not going to be completed by the agreed upon date, the team member needs to see the leader about this prior to the next meeting and establish a new date. This needs to be a team rule, a "nonnegotiable." After a while, getting things done in a timely fashion will become routine.

Holding Down Turnover

When a company goes Lean people often feel they're having to work harder than before, because they are producing more parts. The truth is they don't spend any more time working than they did in the past. But before going Lean, a lot of their time was wasted. For example, they may have had to go somewhere to get materials. Or they had to go somewhere else to get the tools they needed. Every time they moved around to get something, they were not spending time adding value to a product. They were taking time off from a repetitive job. After the transition they will find they're spending most of their time adding value and it may seem as though they are working harder. The truth is they aren't. Even so, they may feel they are.

The solution is to have people rotate jobs. When people change the job they are doing, they "rest" from what they were doing before.

Regularly rotating jobs can help keep morale up and people from leaving the company. In addition, rotating jobs is especially important in a highly variable environment for a practical reason. It's important for people to be multi-skilled so they are able to change jobs as may be required by the constantly changing mix of products being built to customer order. Markets change. Takt times change. And this means people must change the station where they work and the job they normally do.

Another aspect of the Lean transformation is how to deal with personnel who are afraid of the changes to come. Change is a fact of life. But some people will always be comfortable with the situation they are in and resist any change being made to it. This is a situation in which an industrial psychologist can assist in converting good employees into enthusiastic supporters of new ideas and processes and help them embrace the changes the company is going to put in place. The role of the person responsible for Human Resources* for the company is of critical importance It is the HR person's role to keep a hand on the pulse of the organization and to advise the leaders on actions to be taken to keep the transformation running smoothly.

On the Job Training

Almost without question, people will have to be trained to perform new jobs. The way to do this is to put the trainee next to a person who knows the job well. The experienced person can then demonstrate how it's done. After a time, the roles should be reversed. The trainee needs to do the job while the experienced worker watches. In addition, standardized graphical work instructions can be an effective tool to assist and speed up the training of new personnel.

No one should be put into the line until he or she is trained in this way. An important consideration is that the trainee and the trainer should not work at the same time. One should work and the other watch until the new person is up to speed. Two people working at the same time at the same location most likely will interfere with one another. One may need to wait until the other finishes something or he may need to wait for a tool the other operator is using. The result is inefficiency. Moreover, if the trainer works at the same time as the trainee, he or she has no way to see if the trainee is performing the work properly.

The Role of Human Resources

The role of human resources is important in the transformation. The people in HR need to evaluate where the company's culture now stands and, in conjunction with top management, to identify where it needs to be. Then they need to devise a plan to get there.

There is no doubt about it. Many companies today still operate in the autocratic, command and control mode. Such a culture is typical of an industrial company. To be successful in a build-to-order world, however, will require a participative culture in which workers make decisions, to a certain extent manage themselves and feel a strong sense of accountability for what they do. It will also mean training to promote Lean thinking.

HR needs to lay out a path to transform the company into such a culture. realizing that it won't be easy and will take time. It will almost surely require a training program with the objective of transforming command and control managers into coaches who foster participation and initiative on the part of workers. They must become motivators who encourage the team to which they are assigned. A methodical, planned and programmed approach will be required. It is not something that can be done once and then it's finished.

Training will almost certainly have to be conducted at regular and frequent intervals and be ongoing so that Lean thinking, taking initiative and looking for ways to improve and solve problems the moment they arise becomes ingrained. There also may be a need for product knowledge training, cross-training to help workers become multi-skilled as well as other functional training.

HR people also need to have their ears to the ground, to understand what's happening and to advise personnel at different levels of the organization concerning what they need to do to achieve objectives. If the HR department is incapable of this it may be necessary to bring in industrial psychologists from the outside to facilitate the transition.

Changing the Company's Structure

The structure of the participative company ultimately needs to be different than that of the command and control organization. The latter will have an organization chart laid out in the traditional hierarchical pyramid. But the Lean, participative organization will operate through interlocking, empowered teams. This is not, however, a change that can be or should be made overnight. It needs to happen over time — to be evolutionary rather than revolutionary.

At least two methods exist for implementing major change. The common approach is called the "define and convince" model, in which an assigned expert (or expert team) defines the change specifics and convinces the rest of the organization to follow a blueprint. This model works best in small companies, largely because of the close link between the company's leadership and its workers. But in large companies, the process is slow, seldom wins widespread buy-in, and often requires extensive infrastructure and procedural controls to maintain the change.

The other method is the "participative model." The leader defines change goals and challenges for the work force to define and execute the changes. The actual process involves a series of facilitated large-group sessions for convergence and decision-making, positioned around smaller group activities. This is where the testing and learning takes place. This approach works best because rapid assimilation of knowledge and buy in usually takes place across the organization. Nevertheless, old line managers often hesitate to use it because it requires the leaders to trust workers with the details instead of people they perceive as experts.

Participative change roles are quite different from those in the design-and-convince approach. Leaders are not order givers but participants in learning and decision-making. Experts don't define specific changes, they provide substantive knowledge. Workers are not 'change targets,' but full participants in learning and decision-making.

Leaders ought to set targets and make strategic decisions. The people who will have to live with the details comprise the group that ought to determine the details. If they do, they will make sure the new system works. And if things aren't working, they will be motivated to make the modifications necessary to get everything on track.

Administrators aren't needed to control the process or define the results. To make sure change happens in a timely fashion, milestones need to be set that will mark key points of system integration. These large group sessions are forums for defining, understanding and decision-making on major integration issues.

Communicating company goals to all employees allows every person to know how far from or how close he or she is to the objective.

Change Decision Making

In traditional businesses, decisions for a new system are typically made by a few experts and handed down from the top. But in the method suggested here, most change decisions are made at group meetings with the help of facilitators trained in gaining consensus. Things should run smoothly if alternatives are worked out ahead of time by small groups who represent the whole, provided these groups are headed by leaders who have the respect of others. If those affected by changes are active participants in the design of the changes, they will work hard and persevere through the many hiccups that are likely to be encountered along the journey to a new way of working.

Maintain Focus and Enthusiasm

As with any other major project a company undergoes, an important aspect is for top management to maintain focus on it and to project enthusiasm for a successful Lean transformation and the changes that are occurring. Employees should not be allowed to deviate from the goals that have been set forth.

Many leaders of companies know the frustration that results when projects are started and not completed. We have seen projects stall even when excellent results had been achieved up to that point. In some cases, a transformation has not moved beyond the production area. This often happens because day to day activities appear to be more important, especially when resources are tight. An angry customer may call, material may be delayed and so on. Just about anything can seem more important than the action reports and the activities that must be completed for the Lean transformation to take place. In these cases, management needs to hold fast to the Lean vision and continue to picture how the company should be. Otherwise it will face a very real risk of delay and lost momentum. Unfortunately, it can be very difficult to get back that momentum.

Even if activities are performed as called for and required, the most difficult part of the Lean transformation can be to keep enthusiasm at a sufficient level. It is easy to slide into old habits, and go back to the usual way of doing things. That is why "change" should become a normal way of life.

Recap

Management by fear and intimidation is the biggest impediment to a Lean transformation. Since the culture of a company starts at the top, the top leader of an organization must be committed to change. He or she must walk the walk and talk the talk.

No two transformations are the same, even though the processes may be identical. Consistent and ongoing training will likely be required for change in the culture to take place and this will take time. But it can be done. HR should devise a plan in conjunction with top management. This may include product and skills training as well as leadership training.

Action reports may be required for people to accept accountability. An action report, which is distributed after a meeting, zeros in on the decisions made as well as the actions to be taken and who is to take them. Meetings should begin with a review of action reports. Those who were to take action should be called upon for an update. Meetings end with a recap of decisions made, actions to be taken and who is to take them. When people fail to perform under such conditions they are subject to the scrutiny of peers and will usually fall into line quickly.

The Lean organization consists of interlocking teams rather than a hierarchical pyramid, but transforming to this often takes time. Participative change usually works more effectively than the "design and convince" method. This means leaders ought to set targets and make strategic decisions and the people who will have to live with the details ought to determine those details. When this happens those responsible will make sure the system works or be motivated to make modifications to get things on track.

Chapter Six: Measuring Your Lean Transformation

We measure everything in our world today. Students receive grades, TV shows have ratings and baseball players have batting averages. These measures allow us to evaluate the relative success of things that are important to us. And measuring also serves to focus attention on these things. Simply by doing so, we can cause them to improve. A Lean Enterprise is no different. Without having the value of reference, it is impossible to understand the impact of the actions a company has undertaken. In general, process changes that are not measured will not improve, but when a light is shined on an area, something positive tends to happen.

The Kaizen Process

In a Lean transformation, we typically use the kaizen process to transform each area in which we work. Using this process, we eliminate non-value added activities while making value added activities flow. This involves taking a small area, measuring "before" we implement changes, implementing Lean transformation changes, and measuring the results. The process is repeated until the measurements match the goals we've set for the transformation. And since we subscribe to the continuous improvement concept of Lean, this "measure-change-repeat" cycle never stops.

During the kaizen process things typically measured are

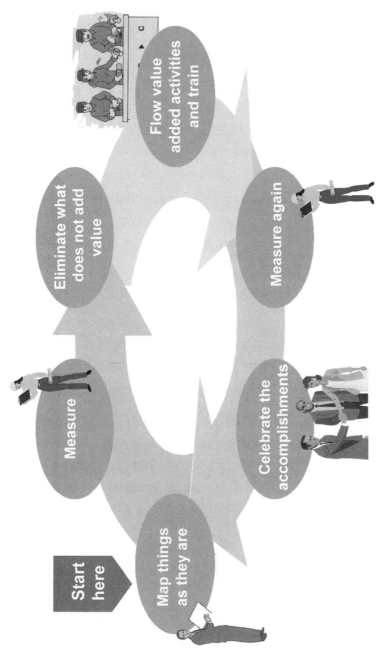

Fig. 21 — Basic Kaizen "measure - change - repeat" cycle

work in process, floor space, throughput or cycle time compared to takt time, labor hours, productivity, line balance,
transportation time and distance between material and people.

We could refer to these measures as "micro-level" measures. They measure each area being transformed. In theory,
as we improve each area of the facility through the Lean
transformation process, the overall results of the business
will improve. But theory is one thing and reality is another.
We also measure the overall effectiveness of the entire Lean
transformation process to insure that the cumulative effect
of each of the individual kaizens has improved the overall
performance of the business. This being the case, we also
need "macro-level" measurements of the business itself.

Three Considerations for Measurements at the Macro Level

Often, businesses already have "macro-level" measures in
place. They exist to support corporate or board goals that
have been set and handed down throughout the organization. Frequently they exist to be used as "objective" measurements as part of the employee compensation system.
Many of these goals or measurements are consistent with
Lean Enterprise measurements, such as inventory turns.
Sometimes, however, they may not be consistent. Goals and
measurements such as manufacturing efficiency, head count,
or unit cost come to mind.

Three things should be kept in mind when determining

what to measure. First, it is important to measure the right things. It's important to fully understand that when management sets overall company goals and links them to compensation, management has set in motion forces that will determine the behavior of workers and staff. It's common in companies where the overriding objective is "efficiency," for example, that people at all levels will focus on efficiency to the detriment of other potentially positive outcomes. In such a company it's common that customer service, including on time delivery, customization, and so forth, suffers. Any activity that would lessen the chance of achieving the stated "efficiency goal" will be sidestepped or postponed.

Second, the level of detail to measure must be determined. In general, it's best to keep all of these measurements at the business level. When corporate measures are cascaded down to individual product lines or departments, they often lose their effectiveness. For example, a product line's leaders may work to get support personnel correctly allocated to another product line in order to improve their own cost picture. There is certainly nothing wrong in allocating overhead properly, but this does nothing to improve the results of the business overall. The cost picture of one product line will improve, and the cost picture of another will take a hit with a sum zero effect. It may be important in some instances to drill down into product lines or some other sub-level to enable a proper analysis of the different segments of a business, but this is probably not what management had in mind. By keeping measurements at the business level, everyone will stay focused on the results of the entire business rather than solely on their particular area of responsibility to the possible detriment of others.

Third and last, measurements need to be simple and easy to get. They should not involve a cumbersome gathering and calculating process.

An important reason for having certain measurements is to establish goals and objectives that management wants to achieve, including a clear timetable for achieving them. Once such goals and objectives are attained it is also important to celebrate the achievements with all personnel involved. This motivates the entire organization and indicates to them that the whole company cares about reaching target objectives and recognizes efforts made.

Types of Macro Level Measurements

What are the appropriate "macro-level" measures of a business that can accurately measure and bring about improvement in the performance of the business? Which ones will also measure the cumulative effect of the Lean transformation process? Also, to what level of detail should these measures be cascaded in order to insure that behavior at the cascaded levels results in improvement in the business overall?

Below is our proposed list of macro level measurements that we think should be kept under control when assessing success of the Lean transformation.

Productivity

1. Total Units Sold or Produced (Normalized into Equivalent Units)/Total Labor Hours. In a highly variable, seasonal environment, the total equivalent units to total labor hours may be the best measurement. Obtaining the equivalent unit may be accomplished by using the standard time established for each of the products and relating this to the reference product. It is important that the calculation consider all labor hours used, including every single human resource working in the business. If detail into a specific product line is desired, simple, manual Activity Based Costing may be used to have a more adequate view of a particular business segment.

2. Total Units Sold or Produced (Normalized Into Equivalent Units)/Direct Labor Hours. In this case as in the prior one, in a highly variable, seasonal environment a need exists to consider production units rather than units sold.

Operational

3. Inventory Turns ($ Sold or $ of COGS/$ of Total Inventory). This is a key measurement of the achievements in a Lean transformation. The reason is that a Lean company produces what is required by the customer when the customer needs it and not before. Suppliers provide products just in time to the company's demand. Quality is included in the production process and is not controlled at the end of it. These elements result in lower inventory, and as such, the

Leaner the company, the higher the inventory turns will be.

In highly variable and seasonal environments, it may make more sense to measure $ produced or $ of COGS produced to $ of total inventory. Special consideration needs to be given to evaluating the results and trends because in highly seasonal environments standard products may be produced in advance since demand at certain times of the year may exceed actual capacity. It may also be the case that instead of producing finished goods, subassemblies are built in advance, i.e., up to the first level of customization.

4. Speed. The time it takes from arrival of an order to delivery. This measurement takes on a different meaning, however, in a highly variable as well as a seasonal environment. In highly seasonal environments the measurement deals with the last or last few customizations rather than the overall process in many cases. It may be that a more adequate measurement is that of on-time-delivery. In repetitive cases, however, the time it takes from "order-to-production-to into-the-hands-of-the-customer" is an indicator of progress made. In highly variable environments an issue is the amount of engineering a product may require and the impact this may make on the overall elapsed time from order to delivery. In these environments, the ability to react to customer needs is an indication of speed of response. A trend needs to show that the various processes involved have been optimized by taking out most of the non-value added activities.

5. On-Time Delivery. The objective is to measure the trend with an ultimate objective of reaching 100% on-time delivery to customers' want dates. Monthly information is presented in a rolling 12 month chart. A month is added and deleted each month. The graph may have a horizontal line representing the goal for the year (i.e. 95%). Some people may want to measure on-time shipment instead of on-time delivery. This is all right if the terms are FOB Shipping Point where the title transfers at the company's dock and the customer pays for the freight. If the terms are FOB Destination, where title transfers on their dock and the supplier pays for the freight, then it should be the delivery date.

In cases where there is an order for perhaps 1,000 pieces and 900 are delivered on-time and 100 are late, this measurement could be 90% since 90% of the parts ordered were delivered on-time. Or it could be zero percent since the order was not delivered complete, on-time. An analysis needs take place to determine what is meaningful for the business.

Manufacturing Cost

6. Conversion Cost (all costs except direct material). This measurement includes all personnel and other costs associated with the production and delivery of a product in the total process from order to delivery.

7. Conversion Cost/Some Operating Base (Units Sold or Produced). In some cases, there's no need to have this measure. In the case of some of our clients, however, where growth is substantial and sustainable, the conversion cost rises in total. But as a percentage of a reference (equivalent units made, dollars produced, et cetera) it goes down. In highly variable and/or seasonal environments, it may make more sense to refer to units produced than units sold. In these cases, expenses are in line with the production strategy rather than with actual sales, which are seasonal.

Purchasing Cost

8. Direct Material percentage (either of Product Cost or of Sales). This is an interesting measure, but it should be kept in mind that the need exists to clearly understand what a trend may actually indicate. In cases of strong economic growth, for example, inflationary pressures on material costs can distort this indicator. Careful analysis is advisable before conclusions are made.

Quality

9. PPM Defective Units. The objective depends on the industry you are working in. Some businesses use the Six Sigma definition, where the goal is 3.4 ppm. This means a production is practically perfect. This is the case for businesses that are closely connected to safety, such as water distribution, airplanes, and so forth. Of course, luggage delivery is far from that objective (think that: every 1,000 passengers traveling in the whole world, 11.4 (1.14% or 11,400 ppm) receive their luggage late, 1.8 (0.18% or 1,800 ppm) receive their luggage damaged, and 0.46 never receive it. In Italy, every 1,000 passengers, 13.3 receive their luggage late). If the current amount of defects you are experiencing is in the range of few percentage points it means your ppm rate is at least 10,000. For some businesses being at that level represents lost sales of spare parts.

Others

10. Profit. We do not want to dwell on this measure. Each company determines its own objectives.

11. Space measured against some operating base (units, $). It is important to understand the use of space before and after the Lean transformation. After the transformation, the use of space should be reduced or the volume produced with the same space should be increased.

There are two last points that should be kept in mind about these measurements. First, where applicable, our recommendation and preference is to measure percentages against sales rather than production so that there is no incentive to create inventory. Second, in all cases, it is important to calculate monthly values and then to show them in a graphical manner in order to assess a trend over time. The trend is what is important. Numerical values can be distorted depending on parameters and definitions. If the trend shows continuous progressive improvement, then the Lean transformation is meeting its goals. Otherwise, these measurements provide an opportunity to review progress made and to take corresponding corrective action. Once implemented, these measurements will provide a meaningful method to insure that the Lean transformation is meeting its goals and that the business as a whole is enjoying tangible benefits.

Pay for Performance

We've found one thing that's true in just about any business. You get what you measure and you pay for. When peoples' jobs and livelihoods depend on something getting done, it almost always gets done. This means it's important to keep score in order to know precisely how the business is doing, and to hand out rewards to employees when the goals they've been given are met. That's why management might consider tying a percentage of everyone's compensation to achieving company goals.

Careful attention needs to be given, however, to the measurements a company uses to reward employees. These will determine employee behavior. One client used "efficiency" as the reward measurement. As a result, operations personnel would produce work orders that gave them high efficiency but they left untouched those that did not help their performance according to the definition of "efficiency" in use. In this case, efficiency depended on standards that did not necessarily reflect the time required to build certain products.

Studies have shown that not everyone in the typical

company is working to move the ball forward. A recent one we saw indicates that about 25 percent of employees are actively engaged and working the way management would like and hope. About 50 percent are neutrally engaged. They represent warm bodies. They come to work, muddle along, and don't do any damage to the company. But the scary part of this study said that about 25 percent of the workforce is actively working against the company. You might label this group "disgruntled." They could be stealing from the company, involved in fraud, or in any of a number of counterproductive activities.

The Story of Nucor Steel

One company, Nucor Steel, has found a way to deal with this. What Nucor has done is tie a big percentage of employees' and managers' compensation directly to steel output and the quality of that output. Nucor's management is aware that for employees, compensation is where the rubber meets the road.

An experienced steelworker at steel companies other than Nucor can easily earn $16 to $21 an hour. At Nucor the guarantee is closer to $10. But consider this. A bonus system that's tied to the number of batches of defect-free steel produced by the shifts an employee works can triple that worker's take-home pay.

Nucor gave out more than $220 million in profit sharing and bonuses to the rank and file in 2005. What did that mean to the average Nucor steelworker? He or she took home nearly $79,000. Plus, a $2,000 one-time bonus to mark the company's record earnings in 2005 and almost $18,000, on average, in profit sharing can be added to that $79,000 average pay check.

But that's only part of the story. At Nucor, not only is good work rewarded, but bad work is penalized. Bonuses are calculated on every order and paid out every week. If workers make a bad batch of steel, and catch it before it has moved on, they lose the bonus they otherwise would have made on that shipment. But if it gets to the customer, they lose three times the amount.

Steel plant workers at Nucor aren't the only ones with a big percentage of their pay at risk. The take-home pay of managers depends heavily on results as well. Department managers typically get a base pay that's 75% to 90% of the market average. But in a great year, that same manager might get a bonus of 75% or even 90% of his base pay, depending on the return on assets of the whole plant.

This adds up to managers and workers who think like and act like owners of the business — rather than workers who are there to put in their time so they can pick up a paycheck. When workers act like owners, good things happen for the business and its shareholders. The proof is in the results. Nucor had sales of $12.7 billion in 2005, up from $4.6 billion in 2000. In 2005, net income was $1.3 billion, up from $311 million in 2000. The value of the company's stock increased 387 percent during the 2000 through 2005 period. This puts rust-belt-industry Nucor ahead of such New Economy icons such as Amazon.com, Starbucks, and eBay.

Recap

We normally use the kaizen process to transform each area in which we work, eliminating non-value-added activities while making value-added activities flow. This involves taking a small area, measuring "before" we implement changes, implementing Lean transformation changes, and then measuring the results. The process is repeated until the measurements match the goals we've set for the transformation. And since we subscribe to the continuous improvement concept of Lean, this "measure-change-repeat" cycle never stops. We typically measure things such as work in process, floor space, throughput or cycle time compared to takt time, labor hours, productivity, line balance, transportation time and distance of material and people.

These are "micro-level" measures of each area being transformed. As each area of the facility improves, the overall results of the business should improve, but nevertheless, we also measure the overall effectiveness of the entire Lean transformation process to insure that the cumulative effect has improved the overall performance of the business.

Three things should be kept in mind when determining what macro-level measurements to take. When management sets overall company goals and links them to compensation, management has set in motion forces that will determine the behavior of workers and staff. If the objective is simply "efficiency," for example, people at all levels will likely focus on efficiency to the detriment of things that may be equally important such as customer service.

Second, the level of detail to measure must be determined. We've found it's best to keep all of these measurements at the business level. When corporate measures are cascaded down to individual product lines or departments, a product line's leaders may work to improve their own cost picture to the possible detriment of the overall operation.

Third, measurements need to be simple and easy to get. They should not involve a cumbersome gathering and calculating process.

Types of Macro-Level Measurements include productivity, speed from order to delivery, on-time delivery, manufacturing cost, purchasing cost and quality.

We've found one thing that's true in just about any business. You get what you measure and you pay for. When peoples' jobs and livelihoods depend on something getting done, it almost always gets done. This means it's important to keep score in order to know precisely how the business is doing, and to hand out rewards to employees when the goals are met. That's why management might consider tying a percentage of everyone's compensation to achieving company goals.

Chapter Seven: Key Factors for Lean Enterprise Success

It's been our experience throughout the world in the many Lean transformations we've been part of, that five factors are required for a successful, ongoing transformation:

(1) Top management team must have a strategic vision of what the organization is moving toward and will become. This team must be able to see how the company will be different, and what, for example, the primary advantages over competition will be. This strategic vision must be held firmly in mind and communicated to leaders and employees throughout an organization so that it becomes a shared vision all are working toward.

(2) Strong line leadership people must be selected as change agents by the primary team. They will head cross-functional teams that guide the transformation. It's essential these individuals be committed to the change. Leaders of the transformation must be chosen carefully. They must have the imagination necessary to grasp "what can be," and share the primary team's vision of the company's future. An important aspect of the makeup of leaders selected to institute change should be that they focus on the future and the possibilities it holds, rather than on the past and its time-honored traditions.

(3) Expert training and support likely will be needed in order to

BUILD TO ORDER

get started. This may require bringing in a seasoned Lean transformation expert to help in at least the initial Lean transformation start up and training phase. After training has taken place and the rollout hs been successful, those left in charge should have enough knowledge to be self-correcting in the event that the transformation strays off course. It also may help to have a sounding board, someone who has been through transformation, who can be called upon periodically for advice and counsel.

(4) Aggressive Lean Enterprise performance targets and tracking are needed. As discussed in the last chapter, people need to know what's expected of them, and they need goals and objectives to shoot for. This might take the form of specific objectives to do with reductions in throughput time, inventory turns, scrap reduction, and returns due to defects. Goals in general can be important motivators, as discussed in the previous chapter.

(5) Impatience by management to see the organization move ahead and deliver tangible results. Impatience means that foot-dragging will not be tolerated. It means that what we often refer to as "concrete heads" will not be given much time to get on board. In its most productive form, impatience should translate into a fire that is lit under the organization to realize the vision.

Indeed, many have discovered what is now referred to as "The Lean Enterprise Paradox." This is that management must be simultaneously directive and empowering. It would seem that these traits do not go hand in hand. But experience has revealed that strong leadership is required — leadership that is unambiguous, leadership that is clear about the Lean Enterprise path. At the same time, a leader must continually empower teams along the way. Teams must be handed complete authority to carry out assigned tasks. Those who would block progress by trying to hold on to the old hierarchy — their turf — and perpetuate an "us versus them" mentality need to be converted. They deserve a chance to move through the five stages of change — denial, anger, bargaining, depression, acceptance — but they cannot be allowed to hold up progress long. There may come a point, if they are stuck in stage one, two, three or four, when the only intelligent course will be to turn them out to pasture.

We have seen that when the five Lean Enterprise factors are present, and obstructionists have been removed, impressive results will be achieved. But if one or more factors are missing, a company's Lean transformation is likely to fail to live up to expectations.

A word of caution is appropriate. Impatience, while needed and potentially constructive, should be tempered with a healthy dose of realism. An important decision to make is how quickly to move ahead once a Lean transformation has begun. In manufacturing and assembly operations, this will depend largely on the ability of the supporting infrastructure to keep up. If one or two lines are all that's involved, infrastructure may not be an issue. But the situation can be considerably different if there are 6, 10, 20, or more assembly lines in a given complex. Maintenance and material handling are likely to become stressed as the conversion of one line after another takes place.

Factor Number One: A Strategic Vision

Here is an important question for the top leader of an organization to ask and answer. Knowing what you now know about Lean Enterprise, what would you want your company to look like if you were starting today from scratch? If you were running a computer company, for example, would your vision be that of Dell, with its ability to customize each order and to produce in a continuous flow to customer pull method of supply, manufacturing, and distribution set up? Or would your vision be modeled after one of the more traditionally run sales and assembly businesses?

If the answer is Dell, how does the Dell model translate to your industry? How would you set it up?

This may well be your vision. To realize it may require dramatic change, and change can be difficult. It can be frightening for those who find comfort in the known and the expected, even when the known and expected are not all that wonderful. Maybe this is why incumbent politicians often have a big advantage over challengers. Given this reality, how can a leader get people to accept the new vision? What will get their attention and blast them out of complacency?

One catalyst can be a real or perceived crisis. It might be

your company no longer is able to compete effectively. Let's look directly into the eyes of reality. Over time, organizations can become over staffed. Positions that once served a useful purpose may become outmoded by changes in technology or the marketplace. Yet the people who fill them remain on the payroll. Unless you happen to be starting an organization from scratch, it is very likely your organization has too much fat, too much waste, too many workers, too much duplication and too much equipment devoted to activities that do not create value. This is doubly true if a competitor happens to adopt a course of Lean transformation. If a company has not yet reached a state of crisis, its leaders would be wise to consider trumping one up. If they wait, they will likely face a real crisis later that will be nearly impossible to overcome.

Not long ago, for example, General Motors announced a major reorganization entailing the elimination of thousands of jobs. If it were not for the magnitude of this overhaul, it's doubtful the story would have created headlines at all, at least not in newspapers beyond the company's headquarters city, Detroit. In this new age of global competition, only those companies offering the highest quality at the lowest prices will survive.

If your company happens to be in what appears to be a do-or-die position, you may actually be fortunate and not yet realize it. An opportunity has presented itself. A catalyst for change is at your fingertips, one that will light a fire under every manager and worker who wants to remain gainfully employed. A build-to-order, Lean Enterprise is a survival strategy they should thankfully embrace, a potential lifesaver they cannot afford to reject. Once they see it this way, most will pull together to do what's necessary to make the transformation, and the odds are excellent that the company will emerge stronger and more competitive.

What if your business doesn't face an immediate crisis? What if the transformation is primarily a defensive measure to remain competitive, or an offensive measure to strengthen the company's position? Opposition will be strong, not from workers, but from middle management.

Those who have been through a transformation will tell you the attitudes of workers will likely change from somber or glum to enthusiastic and upbeat in a matter of days or weeks. Post transformation surveys indicate they often believe that they aren't working as hard afterward as they did before. Employee job satisfaction usually soars. Workers feel empowered because they are.

Factor Number Two: Strong Line Leadership

Strong line leadership — those chosen as team leader change agents — is absolutely critical to a successful Lean Enterprise program. Without their full commitment, failure is almost certain. As has been discussed, becoming a Lean Enterprise involves major cultural change, and this requires perseverance. And cultural and technical roadblocks are not all that must be cleared away. Floor layouts, people, multiple levels of bureaucracy, systems such as accounting and MRP, all will have to be changed. The truth is, Lean Enterprise "goes against the grain" of just about everything companies that have been using the mass manufacturing production model have held dear.

This is one of the most critical lessons learned: The inertia factor of a traditional manufacturer should not be underestimated. For those who do not want to change, it will be a classic case of, "You can lead a horse to water, but you can't make it drink." The truth is, more than inertia is at work. The traditional organization will fight back.

Let's say a successful kaizen event is held with huge improvements in performance. Enthusiasm will be high among the participants. They will be charged up and ready to find more ways to improve. This is probably the moment a backlash from the traditional organization will occur.

Why? Turf has been threatened. In a factory that's gone Lean, it's the old line supervisors who are likely to rebel. You can expect them to complain that, to the great detriment of the company, control and discipline have been lost. A "tug of war" between early adapters and what many have called "concrete heads" will ensue. About 80% of the organization will be caught in the middle. The outcome will either be success or failure, and this will depend on the actions taken by team-leader change agents.

You may recall the example we gave in an earlier chapter

about the autocratic leader who made all the decisions and dressed down subordinates in public. As you can imagine, the workers in this factory were at first very anti-management and pro-union. As we conducted Lean training in this plant, the people seemed perplexed. Nevertheless, we continued on and decided to begin by converting a single line. When the day came to implement the changes, we were surprised that the workers did not seem to be able to reach their new goal. If anything, they appeared to be intentionally sabotaging their own efforts. After few days of observation, we realized that the people were simply not going to reach the goal until the union agreement that was in place was changed. This agreement called for a smaller amount of output than the new goal, and when the old amount was reached the workers stopped. The root of the problem was resentment toward the General Manager. Things did finally change, of course. After a new manager was brought in, the union contract was re-negotiated.

The Lean Enterprise Paradox

This leads to what was referred to a short time ago as the "Lean Enterprise Paradox." Management style must be both directive and empowering.

The words "directive" and "empowering" do not sound as if they ought to go together. In this case they do. Strong leadership is required, leadership that is crystal clear about the Lean Enterprise path and on board with it. At the same time, the top leaders in the organization must continually empower the teams along the way. The best advice is not to waste time with people who will not change. Moreover, be aware that you have a big problem on your hands if many of your plant managers fall into this category, and even a bigger one if you have a concrete head in a general manager position. All probably will have to be replaced, or transformation at the plant level will be stifled. Even if everyone else other than these leaders wants to change, the effort will fail.

Factor Number Three: Expert Training and Support

Expert training and support will likely be required in order for you to get going, especially if little Lean Enterprise experience exists in your company. You may have to bring in someone from the outside to help with this.

But don't go overboard. You will need enough to get started, and enough knowledge on site on an ongoing basis to be self-correcting when a false step or a mistake is made.

Where does the required Lean expertise come from? Typically, it comes from people already on staff, as well as new hires who have prior experience with Lean. It can also come from an outside consultant.

It makes sense to begin the transformation in the area closest to the customer. In manufacturing, this is final assembly. But it could also be the sales organization. Begin the training program with the personnel who work in the selected area. A major goal is to develop a "picture" of a Lean producer in their minds.

Factor Number Four: Aggressive Performance Targets

Measurements are important in tracking Lean Enterprise implementation. They can be designed to take advantage of existing plant-level data and to minimize the amount of additional information to be collected. As covered in the last chapter, some main indicators are and might include: inventory turns, defects per thousand (customer PPM), on-time-delivery (OTD) to customer want dates, and financial performance measures such as SG&A (Sales, General & Administrative overhead). Our book, *Lean Transformation* (Oaklea Press, 1999), goes into detail on each one of the various types of metrics mentioned above that might be tracked, and clearly explains how to read and monitor them.

Factor Number Five: Impatience

Impatience should lead the Lean Enterprise leader to take action when he or she begins hearing, "You don't understand. We are different." Or, "If we do that, it will disrupt the organization." Impatience means that concrete heads will not be given much time to get on board.

Top leaders need to take at least a daily walk through the organization. They need to hand out positive strokes where progress is apparent and express displeasure with a lack of results.

The primary (top) team in an organization should demonstrate impatience by regularly reviewing progress, and make it known they know exactly where things stand. A positive trend, or the lack of one, should be noted. If you move too slowly in transforming to Lean, valuable momentum and enthusiasm can be lost. If you move too quickly, inevitable glitches, and the inability of materials supply and maintenance to keep up, can give nay sayers gasoline to pour on the fire of discontent. Count on it. There will be nay sayers.

Communications

And finally, communications can play an important role in helping the organization jell and rally to accomplish the Lean transformation. Leaders should use every tool they can, from newsletters, to strategy documents, to brochures, videos and advertising, in order to spread the word and turn up the heat. Nothing makes something so real as putting it in writing. An ad or story in your industry's trade journal that talks about your going Lean signals that you're deadly serious, not only to customers, but to employees. So what if your competitors find out what you're up to? By the time they get around to trying to copy you, you'll be light years ahead of them.

In Conclusion

Chances are you picked up this book because you believe high customization, low cost, quick turnaround, and ever diminishing volumes is the future. If your company can achieve these goals, it will have an important competitive advantage. After all, specialized products generally cost significantly more than standard models off the shelf. But by using Lean manufacturing techniques, this no longer has to be the case. Whatever your industry, whether it be automotive, apparel, electronics, consumer products, white goods, industrial products, or anything in between, the issues are similar and so are the solutions. We hope this book has given you a good picture of this and what can be done.

Perhaps you feel the effort required to become a Lean manufacturer is overwhelming. But think about this. The options are limited for companies facing the issues described in the in the opening paragraphs of this book. As you recall, one is to do nothing. Just keep doing what you have been doing and hope for the best. But all it will take are one or two competitors willing and able to offer customization and quick turnaround with comparable quality and prices similar to or lower than yours, and your company could be driven out of business.

As we've traveled the world, we've come to know many businesses that are probably similar to yours. The conclusion we've come to is that in all likelihood the only viable option you have is to transform into a Lean Enterprise. Cost efficiency will improve dramatically. Quality will improve. Lead times will be cut. You will be able to react to the market faster and to offer just what customers want at prices your competitors will find hard to beat.

Sounds good, doesn't it?

If you are not yet convinced, allow us to conclude with something else to think about, the words of the White Rabbit in Lewis Carol's *Alice in Wonderland*:

"In this land you have to run as fast as you can just to stay in the same place."

The race is on. Now's the time to begin.

INDEX

About the Authors

 **Jorge L. Larco** is president of J. L. Larco & Associates, Inc., a consulting firm that provides domestic and international consulting services for manufacturing and service companies. A senior executive with many years of experience in industry, Jorge provides expertise in leading global manufacturing companies and implementing Lean Enterprise techniques, turning around troubled companies, and in the development and implementing of successful business strategies.

Mr. Larco, who is fluent in four languages, is uniquely qualified to help large and small companies. Born in Argentina and a US citizen by choice, he opened his consulting company in 1993, and has has successfully led conversions to Lean Enterprise in such far-flung locations as Italy, France, Brazil, Australia, and New Zealand, as well as the United States. Mr. Larco has also been responsible for designing and developing two electronic board-stuffing facilities for a large customer, that have been designed based exclusively on lean principles and practices. The facilities were developed in record time and with unusually limited resources.

Prior to starting his own consulting business, Mr. Larco was with TRW as VP and General Manager of European Steering Operations in Spain and Italy, and he has held several high-level executive positions with TRW in the USA. He has a M.S. in Electromechanical and Electronics Engineering from the University of Buenos Aires and he is a graduate of the Tuck Executive Program at the Amos Tuck School of Business Administration at Dartmouth.

Mr. Larco is co-author of Lean Transformation, How to Transform Your Business Into a Lean Enterprise (Oaklea Press, 1999), which is currently in its eleventh printing. It has also been published in Italian, German and Chinese. Mr. Larco is also a co-author of a second book, A Workbook for Assessing your Lean Transformation, which is designed for assisting in the periodic evaluation of a Lean Transformation. This book, available in English and Italian, is a practical tool that enables the assessment of the initial lean state, tracking of the transformation to lean, benchmarking against other companies. It also helps facilitate effective communication throughout a company.

Mr. Larco has been a regular lecturer at the a number of universities including the Manufacturing Leaders Programme, Institute of Manufacturing, University of Cambridge, United Kingdom; The Masters Program at the MIB, School of Business, Trieste, Italy; the EMBA program at the University of Trieste, Italy; and the SDA Bocconi, University of Milano, Italy. Mr. Larco speaks English, Spanish, Italian and French.

He can be reached at **jlarco@earthlink.net.**

About the Authors

 **Elena Bortolan** has been involved since 1997 in a diverse and varied number of activities focused on lean enterprise concepts and practices. She has gained an important experience in running and transforming traditional companies into lean producers.

In 1996 she worked as consultant and from January until May 1997 she worked in a jewelry factory. In June 1997, she was hired at Eliwell S.p.A., in Belluno (Italy), an electronic firm part of the Invensys group (a multinational company based in England). As Assistant Production Manager she participated in the initial implementation of Lean Enterprise and becoming Production manager in March 99. In March 2000 she joined the Invensys' group of consultants implementing Lean Enterprise concepts and practices in a number of companies belonging to the group.

From May 2000 she was responsible for starting a new factory in Slovakia, a lean facility designed for the production of electronic boards (Contract Electronic Manufacturing). The project included construction of the facility's building, purchasing and installation of all equipment, hiring and training of all management and direct personnel and, finally, start of production activities. The complete project lasted one year, at the end of which the factory was transferred to the end customer.

Since April 2001 Elena Bortolan has been working as an independent consultant cooperating with the consulting firm J.L. Larco & Associates, Inc. During this period she introduced Lean Enterprise concepts in a number of manufacturing companies in Italy, Mexico, Canada, Romania, Poland, UK, USA, Slovakia, Germany and Malta. Mr. Larco and Ms. Bortolan participated in a project to develop specifications for lean software designed to support lean facilities, for a major software firm. She taught an "Integrated Logistics" course for TV Tecnologia (Treviso Chamber of Commerce, Italy). Elena also taught Advanced Logistics at the Masters program University of Trieste (Italy).

Ms. Bortolan is a graduate of the University of Padova (Italy) with a degree in Management Engineering. In 2004 Elena obtained her MBA from University of Bologna, Italy. Ms. Bortolan speaks Italian, English, Spanish and can communicate in Romanian and Slovakian. She lives in Italy.

Ms. Bortolan can be reached at **bortolan@attglobal.net.**

About the Authors

Michael H. Studley has extensive international work experience in a number of countries, including the USA, Mexico, England, Germany, Italy, Poland, Malta, Egypt, Australia, New Zealand, Thailand, and China. He is a Lean Enterprise professional with a remarkable track record of success in company-wide process improvement campaigns in the areas of Manufacturing, Distribution, Materials, and Administration. A unique combination of backgrounds in Lean Enterprise training and implementation, Operational and Project Finance, and Project Management have enabled him to contribute millions of dollars in process improvement campaigns for recent clients.

Mr. Studley has a unique ability to identify organizational and process waste (costs), identify value, uncover the "hidden factory", estimate turnaround costs, and identify opportunities within manufacturing organizations.

With over 10 years of business experience solving problems, identifying opportunities, and developing Lean business systems that ensure long-term success, Mike understands the importance of properly implementing the Lean principles throughout an organization.

Holds a Masters Degree in Business Administration (MBA) from the University of Central Florida and a Bachelor's Degree in Business Administration with a concentration in Finance from the University of Florida.

He has led company-wide Continuous Improvement activities incorporating all elements of the Lean toolset (JIT, 5S, Visual Management, Six Sigma, Empowered team based continuous improvement programs); has implemented process improvements that reduced labor, scrap, and cycle time while increasing repeatability and overall quality. Mr. Studley has played a key roll in the turnaround of failing manufacturing businesses, has helped established lean "showcase" facilities. Mr. Studley has also been a key player in the management of business consolidations.

He can be reached at **mstudley@attglobal.net**